# Music of the Birds
## A Celebration of Bird Song

*Yellow-headed Blackbird*

# *Music of the Birds*
## *A Celebration of Bird Song*

*Common Yellowthroat*

## Lang Elliott

*with photos and sound recordings*
*by the author and others*

Houghton Mifflin Company

Boston   New York

1999

*Dickcissel*

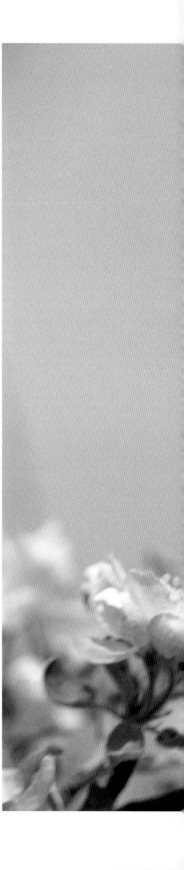

For information about permission to reproduce selections from
this book, write to Permissions, 215 Park Avenue South,
New York, NY 10003

ISBN 0-618-00697-4 (pa)
0-618-00698-2 (cl)

Designed and produced by Lang Elliott,
NatureSound Studio, P.O. Box 84,
Ithaca, New York 14851-0084

First Edition

Printed by C & C Offset, Hong Kong
10  9  8  7  6  5  4  3  2  1

Cover photographs by Lang Elliott
Front cover: Chestnut-sided Warbler
Back cover: Scarlet Tanager, Yellow Warbler, Indigo Bunting
Front cover flap: Sedge Wren

*Northern Parula*

*Yellow Warbler*

# Contents

*Gray Catbird*

# Preface

Creating *Music of the Birds* has been a labor of love. The seed for the book was planted nearly fifteen years ago when I began recording birds to produce audio guides. In bookstores, I found few popular books on bird song and none that focused on the aesthetics of listening—on how to appreciate nature's finest music. To fill this vacuum became my goal. Little did I realize how much work would be involved. Not only did I have to gather sound recordings, I had to produce high-quality photographs of singing birds and find poems and prose to support my theme.

The process of gathering materials was wonderfully educational. I learned to identify bird songs in the process of making recordings. Many times in my travels, I would record a bird in the twilight of dawn, long before I had a chance to see and identify it. Later in the morning, I would run after the singer with binoculars, hoping to get my first view. Taking photographs brought more new experiences. For the first time I saw birds up close and was thrilled to see them shake out their songs with abandon. Discovering and reading poems and natural history prose was also moving—I was pleased beyond measure to find beautiful and revealing words describing the avian musicians that had become so important to my life.

When I began my survey of literature, I made a special effort to uncover sensitive writing that captured the essence of the listening experience—of encountering our native birds singing in natural surroundings. To my surprise and delight, by far the richest source of material was from naturalists and poets of the 1800s and early 1900s, including such famliar names as Thoreau, Burroughs, Emerson, and Whitman, along with a host of other less well known writers. All had a knack for describing the listening experience—their observations were lucid, alive, and timeless, and they freely acknowledged the effect of bird song on their emotions.

The early writers conveyed sentiment so well that I did not see the need to draw upon contemporary poetic works. This is not meant to belittle modern poets, who are evolving new styles, but it gave me the opportunity to celebrate early writers and bring to light their wonderful poems and prose—contributions that could easily be lost with the passing of time. As Liberty Hyde Bailey observed in 1903, "The good New England poets, did they not know nature? Have they not left us the very essence and flavor of the fields and woods and the sky?"

To keep in tune with the times, I consulted numerous contemporary scientific studies that elucidate the biology of bird song. Suffice it to say that my text is illuminated by the painstaking work of hundreds of ornithologists who have uncovered new and useful information. To reduce clutter and maintain the aesthetic and poetic flavor of the book, such studies have not been individually referenced. In my sources section, however, I recommend a number of texts for those who want to explore the science of bird song more deeply.

Now that the book is done, I am pleased at how well the elements fit together. Read through the text at your leisure. Listen to the songs on the disc. Enjoy the photographs. Savor the quotations. And be assured that a world of heightened appreciation awaits you if you go outdoors and embrace the music of the birds. But beware! You may end up like me, waiting impatiently for the snow and ice to melt, listening quietly for the first cheerful notes, and finally celebrating with joy those glorious days when spring has arrived and the birds are in full song.

# Acknowledgments

I am grateful to the following for their expert editing of content and design: Ed Kanze, Dan Otis, Don Kroodsma, Richard Baer, Tom Bennigson, Catherine Landis, and my editors at Houghton Mifflin Company: Harry Foster and Lisa White. In addition, I am beholden to all my dedicated friends who helped me acquire photographs and sound recordings, who contributed poems and quotes about bird song, and who provided me with unfailing emotional support. I offer my deepest gratitude to the early poet-naturalists who felt nature so deeply, to the pioneer American bird song recordists who set the stage for my own work, and to all those who have advanced the art of bird photography through the years. And last, but not least, I applaud the bird musicians themselves, who have given me this unique opportunity to celebrate the extraordinary beauty of their songs.

*Marsh Wren*

*O there's a song on the fragrant breeze,*
*From every bird that sings,*
*And the rapture of their melodies,*
*Through all the welkin rings.*
                    — CLARENCE HAWKES

# Why Birds Sing

*As human beings, we respond emotionally to the voices of birds. We are moved by their varied and musical utterances. Bird songs soothe our spirits and bring joy to our lives. In the songs of birds, we may even hear heavenly voices — healing music from a world outside ourselves. We listen in awe, spellbound by what we hear, and cannot help but wonder why the birds are singing. Are they really making music? Are they singing to us, to one another, or only to themselves?*

The question of why birds sing can be approached from two directions: the scientific perspective, which derives from evolutionary biology, and the poetic perspective, which springs from our emotional experience of hearing birds sing. Superficially, the two viewpoints seem at odds. However, a close look reveals that both yield valid and useful information, and both contribute to the richness of our experience of bird song and, more generally, to the quality of our relationship with nature.

The scientific view focuses on the mechanism by which a bird's behavior evolved. Scientists explore the function or adaptive significance of bird song in an attempt to determine how singing contributes to an individual's reproductive success. Scientists draw conclusions based on close observations of behavior and then scrutinize them within the framework of evolutionary biology. The scientist tends to view himself as an "objective observer" and attempts to describe bird behavior free of emotional and anthropomorphic interpretation, as if he were "an entity outside of nature, looking in."

In contrast, the poet is concerned with feelings and the effects of bird song on human emotions. The poet strives to observe bird behavior closely, but accepts that he is "a part of nature, looking at itself," and hence makes no special attempt to be objective and free of emotion. In fact, the poet focuses primarily on the realm of emotion because that is where most human experience is rooted. The poet is concerned with joy and pleasure, pain and sadness — with the full spectrum of human feelings and how the natural world influences those feelings. Scientific knowledge is important to the poet, but primarily as a springboard from which to leap into the domain of feeling.

*The birds pour forth their souls in notes*
*Of rapture from a thousand throats.*
> — WILLIAM WORDSWORTH

Science provides useful and interesting insights. It tells us that bird songs have evolved as communication signals that transfer information from one individual to others of the same species. A bird's song is usually a complex auditory signal that is musical or songlike to human ears. Among songbirds, only the males typically produce song, and only during the spring and early summer breeding season. Especially at dawn, males repeat song after song from prominent perches, in the absence of obvious stimuli.

Song has several functions. First and foremost, it expresses territory ownership. By singing, a resident male alerts other males of the same species that his territory is occupied and likely to be defended. Song also helps unmated males attract mates. And, once mating has occurred, song helps maintain pair bonds by assuring a female that her mate is nearby and that all is well. The term "bird song" usually refers only to songbirds, but many non-songbirds, such as herons, owls, shorebirds, and woodpeckers, make songlike sounds that have similar territorial and mate-attracting functions.

*Black-capped Chickadee*

*For, what are the voices of birds . . .*
*But words, our words,*
*Only so much more sweet?*
— ROBERT BROWNING

*Black-and-white Warbler*

*Baltimore Oriole*

Songbirds also produce what are known as "calls." This category includes all utterances that cannot be classified as song. Calls are usually simple in structure. Most are given in response to specific stimuli, and calling bouts are usually brief. Calls are often produced by both sexes and by immature as well as mature birds, both during and outside the breeding season. Calls have a variety of functions: there are alarm calls, flocking calls, feeding calls, contact calls, begging calls, aggressive calls, and many others. Given their different qualities and contexts of occurrence, calls are usually quite easy to distinguish from song, although some songbirds have simple, call-like songs.

A bird's repertoire of songs and calls might seem meager when compared to the complexity of human language, but scientific studies show that birds communicate a variety of useful messages with their small number of sounds. Gilbert White, an eighteenth-century English naturalist and poet, arrived at this conclusion through personal observation, writing, "the language of birds is very ancient, and like other ancient modes of speech, very elliptical; little is said, but much is meant and understood." A major goal of the scientist is to study elliptical meaning and determine what is "meant and understood"—what is the communication value of bird sound within the perceptual world of the bird itself.

*The birds I heard [today] sung as freshly as if it had been the first morning of creation.*
— HENRY DAVID THOREAU

*Eastern Towhee*

*Prairie Warbler*

*Indigo Bunting*

*As long as I live, I'll hear
waterfalls and birds and winds sing.*
— JOHN MUIR

*Chipping Sparrow*

*Northern Mockingbird*

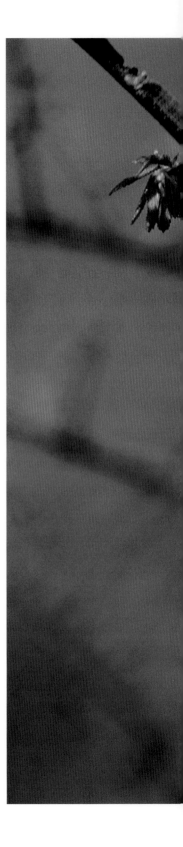

Poets wonder how a bird feels when it sings. Although science tells us that birds sing because song is adaptive and has a useful function in bird society, this does not inform us about the mental or emotional state of a singing bird. There is little reason to believe that a bird is directly aware of the function of its song. Bird song may act as a territorial signal, but a male songbird may sing simply because singing feels good. To determine the actual emotional state of a sound-making bird is probably impossible, even within the framework of modern science. As yet, there is no way for a scientist to enter into a bird's mind and feel its experience. In fact, to do so would break a cardinal rule of scientific objectivity: to be an impartial observer, without feeling. So a great mystery remains. But this mystery opens the door to poetic exploration and interpretation of the mind of the bird.

An important gift of science is that it provides us with a wealth of detailed and repeatable observations that increase our understanding and appreciation of bird song. Science describes the exact structure of songs, it elucidates the song repertoires of individuals and species, it defines the circumstances under which bird song occurs, and it investigates the adaptiveness of all these variations. Woe to the poet who ignores this body of knowledge! Woe to the poet who gets it wrong when it comes to basic natural history, who has no grounding in the earthly reality of scientific fact! The distinguished botanist Liberty Hyde Bailey, in his provocative

*Blue-winged Warbler*

book *The Nature Study Idea* (1903), stated this succinctly: "There can be no objection to the poetic interpretation of nature. It is essential only that the observation be correct and the inference reasonable." In other words, nature poetry should be based on careful observation that is consistent with scientific fact, even if its primary goal is to illuminate the human spirit.

Poets often imagine that the birds are singing directly to us. However, science supports the belief that birds sing only to one another, that their songs function exclusively within the society of the birds. Yet we humans listen with joy and excitement and respond emotionally to what we hear. Many of us sense that, in the grand scheme of things, the birds are singing to us, to the spirit within us, even as they sing among themselves. Perhaps we and they are somehow joined on a spiritual level. Perhaps it is no accident that we are here on earth witnessing the glory of their music. Whatever the truth, is it not our birthright to listen, to enjoy, and to be moved by their songs?

The poet investigates this reaction of the heart and attempts to put the experience into words that are meaningful to others. Perhaps unknowingly, he also points toward a common ground of human experience — a cross-cultural, heartfelt response to the inherent beauty of bird song. In a sense, birds truly do "sing the music of heaven in this world," as sixteenth-century haiku master Kobayashi Issa exclaimed. The poet listens for this music and responds with feeling to what he hears.

> *Hard is the hert that loveth nought,*
> *In May, when al this mirth is wrought,*
> *When he may on these braunches here*
> *The smale briddes syngen clere*
> *Her blesful swete song pitous . . .*
> — GEOFFREY CHAUCER

*White-eyed Vireo*

*Scarlet Tanager (immature male)*

# Nature's Finest Songsters

*We naturally attend to the the most beautiful bird songs that we hear in our surroundings — the songs that please our ears, excite our emotions, and appeal to our aesthetic and musical sensibilities. Poets and naturalists alike seem unanimous in their praise of our finest avian songsters. But why do the songs of these species move us? What is it about their songs that captivates our attention? And is it meaningful to compare bird songs to music created by humans?*

Judging bird songs by musical criteria is perhaps a bit unfair. Music is a human construction, a deliberate attempt to mold sound into a time and frequency pattern that evokes a desired emotional or aesthetic effect. Human music and the playing of musical instruments are relatively new phenomena, created by human beings primarily over the last several thousand years, with immense development and changes in recent times.

Bird song preceded human music. Considered from a scientific perspective, it evolved with the appearance of songbirds during the Pliocene and early Pleistocene periods, several million years ago. While bird song has changed through the ages in response to natural selection, its basic attributes probably developed quickly and it is likely that most of the bird songs we hear today have existed for hundreds of thousands, if not millions, of years, as long as the bird species themselves have been on earth. If we could transport ourselves back to prehistoric times, we might well be greeted by the rollicking song of a robin and the flutey ramble of a thrush, each sounding much the same as they do today.

At the dawn of consciousness, the sounds of nature doubtless stirred the emotions of prehistoric humans. Perhaps responding at first with simple imitations, humans may then have developed primitive forms of music, forging rhythms and beats like those heard in the natural world and embellishing them with whistles and squeaks like those of birds and other creatures. In all the natural world, the songs of birds had the most pleasing melodic themes and variations and probably inspired humans to compose their own melodies and then integrate them with rhythms already created.

*And where the shadows deepest fell,*
*The wood thrush rang his silver bell.*
— HENRY WADSWORTH LONGFELLOW

Thus bird song may have been the original stimulus for the development of musical melodies among humans — the natural template that aroused the first inkling of melodic sensibility and encouraged the evolution of music. Although nature's melodies, especially bird songs, are inherently beautiful, humans still had to create music of their own. For, as Henry Van Dyke so clearly stated in "The Pipes O' Pan" (1909):

> Great Nature had a million words,
> In tongues of trees and songs of birds,
> But none to breathe the heart of man,
> Till Music filled the pipes o' Pan.

If we choose to judge the musicality of a particular bird's song, we concern ourselves with variables such as tonal quality, complexity of songs or song sequences, loudness, and duration of singing, as well as criteria for musicality such as rhythm, melody, unity of organization, themes, and variations. Similarly, when poets praise their favorite bird songs, they often choose adjectives that refer to musical aspects of the songs: sweet, melodious, clear, rich, pure, silvery, bell-like, ringing, flute-like, and so forth. All these are familiar measures of musicalness.

*Hermit Thrush*

Narrowing our focus to our finest native songsters, one bird group stands out above all others: the Thrush family. John Burroughs sums up the situation in *Wake Robin* (1871): "If we take the quality of melody as the test, the wood-thrush, hermit-thrush, and veery-thrush, stand at the head of our list of songsters . . . The emotions excited by the songs of these thrushes belong to a higher order, springing as they do from our deepest sense of beauty and harmony in the world."

The Hermit Thrush is perhaps North America's most highly regarded singer, both for musicality and emotional impact. The hermit's enchanting song begins with a clear whistled note, followed by a rapid flutelike jumble of notes having a ventriloquial quality. Each male has several different song patterns in its repertoire and rarely repeats the same song twice in a row.

Poets and naturalists are united in their praise of the Hermit Thrush's song, describing it variously as tender, serene, wild, ethereal, peaceful, solemn, and ecstatic — adjectives that ascribe an exalted, religious quality to the song. Burroughs thought it an expression of "serene religious beatitude" that embodies "a peace and a deep, solemn joy that only the finest souls may know." The Iroquois believed the Hermit Thrush flew high into the heavens to receive its voice from the spirit world. The melody and cadence of the song is imitated in poetry and prose, with words chosen to convey the reverence that is evoked. Burroughs likened the hermit's song to "O spheral, spheral! . . . O holy, holy!" Whitman (1865) translated it as

*Wood Thrush*

"O liquid free and tender . . . O wild and loose to my soul . . . O wondrous singer."

The emotional impact of the hermit's beautiful song is undoubtedly related to its breeding habitat: dark, cathedral-like forests of hemlock or pine and secluded, swampy stands of cedar, tamarack, or spruce. Only a "hermit" would inhabit such remote places, spinning exalted songs and choosing "thus to fling its soul upon the growing gloom," as poet Thomas Hardy observed in "The Darkling Thrush" (1900). Whitman conveys a similar feeling in "When Lilacs Last in the Dooryard Bloom'd" (1865):

> From deep secluded recesses,
> From the fragrant cedars and the ghostly pines so still,
> Came the carol of the bird.

While the Hermit Thrush ranks high in terms of religious beatitude, the Wood Thrush excites the listener with a brilliant, enchanting strain that truly delights the ear. The song of the Wood Thrush begins with several soft notes followed by a loud and melodious flutelike phrase that terminates with a ringing trill. Each male has perhaps ten or twenty song variants in his repertoire, and he sings one after the other, almost never repeating the same song twice in a row.

*Wood Thrush*

Henry David Thoreau found the Wood Thrush's song to be the most genial to his nature. He wrote in his journal on July 5, 1852: "This bird never fails to speak to me out of an ether purer than that I breathe, of immortal beauty and vigor. He deepens the significance of all things seen in the light of his strain. He sings to make men take higher and truer views of things." Henry Wadsworth Longfellow distilled his experience of hearing a Wood Thrush with poignant verse: "And where the shadows deepest fell, the wood thrush rang his silver bell." John Townsend Trowbridge (1903) shared a similar sentiment:

> Like liquid pearls fresh showered from heaven,
> The high notes of the lone wood-thrush
> Fall on the forest's holy hush.

The songs of the Wood Thrush and Hermit Thrush are similar but have different effects on a listener. F. Schuyler Mathews, author of *The Field Book of Wild Birds and Their Music* (1904), compared the songs of the two species by drawing parallels to compositions by Beethoven. He was reminded of the robust melodies of the *Fifth Symphony* when he heard the Wood Thrush, and of the softer refined beauty of the *Moonlight Sonata* when the Hermit Thrush sang.

*Veery*

Other native thrushes rate high as beautiful singers, especially the Swainson's Thrush and the Veery. The song of the Swainson's Thrush is a flutelike ramble that spirals upward in pitch, with increasingly complex modulations of tone as the song progresses. Each male has about five song types that it sings in a relatively fixed order. The early poets would have been impressed indeed, but most were not familiar with this uncommon denizen of wet bogs, swamps, and thickets in northern and mountainous habitats.

The Veery, a resident of moist woodlands and streamside thickets, has an exquisite, magical song — an ethereal downward spiral of flutey notes, with an echoing, ventriloquial quality. Wilson Flagg, in *A Year with the Birds* (1881), wrote: "When we are in a thoughtful mood, the song of the Veery surpasses all others in tranquilizing the mind and yields something like an enchantment to our thoughts." Frank Chapman, author of *Bird Life* (1897), provides a thoughtful comparison of the Veery's song to those of the other

*Veery*

thrushes: "The Veery's mysterious voice vibrates through the air in pulsating circles of song, like the strains of an Aeolian harp. The Wood Thrush's notes are ringing and bell-like; he sounds the matin and vesper chimes of the day, while the Hermit's hymn echoes through the woods like the swelling tones of an organ in some vast cathedral." Henry Van Dyke ("The Veery," 1897) loved the veery's song so much that he wished it would be his final farewell:

> *And when my light of life is low,*
> *And heart and flesh are weary,*
> *I fain would hear, before I go,*
> *The wood-notes of the veery.*

Two other thrushes with veerylike songs are the Bicknell's and Gray-cheeked thrushes, inhabitants of northern coniferous forests. The two species have nearly identical songs. John Burroughs, in *Riverby* (1894), praised the Bicknell's otherworldly performance, declaring that its song is "more under the breath than any other thrush, as if the bird was blowing in a delicate, slender, golden tube . . . like a musical whisper of great sweetness and power."

All our native thrushes share the habit of singing at dusk. Their twilight performances stand out because most other bird species are silent in the evening. Thoreau was impressed (June 22, 1853): "As I come over the hill, I hear the wood thrush singing his evening lay. This is the only bird whose note affects me like music, affects the flow and tenor of my thought, my fancy and imagination. It lifts and exhilarates me. It is inspiring. It is a medicative draught to my soul. It is an elixir to my eyes and a fountain of youth to all my senses." Emily Tolman wrote a poem focusing on the Hermit Thrush's performance, which she heard both at dawn and dusk:

> *In the deep, solemn wood, at dawn I hear*
> *A voice serene and pure, now far, now near,*
> *Singing sweetly, singing slowly,*
> *Holy; oh, holy, holy;*
>
> *Again at evening hush, now near, now far —*
> *Oh, tell me, art thou voice or bird or star?*
> *Sounding sweetly, sounding slowly,*
> *Holy; oh, holy, holy.*

Walt Whitman refers many times to the twilight song of the Hermit Thrush in his poem "When Lilacs Last in the Dooryard Bloom'd" (1867), written to express his grief over Lincoln's death. Supposedly, John Burroughs provided Whitman with crucial information about the hermit's song. I love the poem's final verse:

*Lilac and star and bird twined with the chant of my soul,*
*There in the fragrant pines and the cedars dusk and dim.*

While the thrushes receive the most attention from the poets, a variety of other native birds have songs with high musical and aesthetic impact. These include several wrens, the mockingbird and its relatives, and a variety of sparrows and finches. And who does not delight each spring in the robust whistled songs of common neighborhood species such as the robin, cardinal, and oriole?

Among the wrens, the Carolina Wren of the East is an energetic singer with a loud, ringing song composed of rapidly repeated phrases. A popular mnemonic device that mimics the cadence of the song is *tea-kettle, tea-kettle, tea-kettle.* Although lacking the exalted, liquid quality of thrush songs, the Carolina Wren gets high marks for loudness, repetition, and variety. Each male has a repertoire of twenty or more different songs — he sings one type many times in a row before finally switching to another.

The Winter Wren is also an exceptional singer. An inhabitant of northern forests and high mountains, this species has an ecstatic, silvery song that may last ten seconds or more. Each song is a rapid series of high-pitched, tinkling notes delivered at a rate of fifteen per second or faster. Naturalists have compared the Winter Wren's song to the tinkling, gurgling, or bubbling sounds made by streams of water. The song reminded Burroughs of "a tremulous, vibrating tongue of silver," and he wrote that "the silence was suddenly broken by a strain so rapid and gushing, and touched with such a wild, sylvan plaintiveness, that I listened in amazement" (1871). Thoreau (July 10, 1858) hailed the "exceptionally brisk and lively strain" of the Winter Wren and was impressed by the song's "incessant twittering flow," that sounded like a "fine corkscrew stream issuing with incessant lisping tinkle from a cork, flowing rapidly."

The Bewick's Wren is another musical singer, with each male having about fifteen songs in its repertoire. Its song pattern resembles that of the Song Sparrow (see page 32). Less musical is the well-known House Wren, who delivers its excited bubbling chatter with great enthusiasm, shaking all over and ruffling its feathers as it sings. A western species with a musical song is the Canyon Wren, whose descending series of loud, plaintive whistles

*Carolina Wren*

*Winter Wren*

echo magically off canyon walls. Ralph Hoffman (1927) described this wren's song as "a cascade of sweet, liquid notes, like the spray of a waterfall in sunshine."

Among the sparrows, we find a number of great singers, my favorites being the Bachman's, Song, Lark, Fox, and White-throated sparrows. The Bachman's Sparrow of the southern pine woods has a beautiful song with a thrushlike quality. The common pattern is a pure, clear whistle followed by a loud, melodic trill. The overall effect is quite musical, partly because the pitch interval between the introductory note and the trill are usually quite pleasing to the ear. Each male has twenty or more songs in its repertoire and often sings two different songs in rapid succession to create an exquisitely beautiful "double-song."

*Bachman's Sparrow*

Common over much of North America, the Song Sparrow enlivens each spring with its energetic outbursts. Songs are a variable sequence of notes, including clear whistles and buzzy sounds. Each male has about ten songs in its repertoire and tends to repeat one pattern for several minutes before changing to another. Although the Song Sparrow does not rank high for sheer musicality, many poets have applauded its song. Ralph Waldo Emerson, probably referring to this species, wrote in "Each and All" (1867): "I thought the Sparrow's note from heaven, singing at dawn on the alder bough." Wilson Flagg (1881), considered the Song Sparrow "the true harbinger of spring; and, if not the sweetest songster, he has the merit of bearing to man the earliest tidings of the opening year, and of proclaiming the first vernal promises of the season . . . the Song Sparrow delights us . . . because he sings the sweet prelude to the universal hymn."

Arthur Allen (1954), in an early audio guide to bird sounds, distilled the essence of the Song Sparrow's performance with friendly, down-home prose: "That's a cheerful little bird, you remark, as a Song Sparrow pipes from the bushes by the roadside. The song is not clear, for it has quite a burr to it, yet it is given with such obvious enthusiasm that you feel it is one of the pleasantest that you've ever heard. *Hip hip hooray boys, that spring is here again,* it seems to say, but its phrases can be as fickle as the weather."

Other sparrows with noteworthy songs include the Lark, Fox, and White-throated Sparrows. The Lark Sparrow's complex song is similar to that of the Song Sparrow, but perhaps more musical. Males have a number of song types in their repertoire and they sing one type after the other, without repeating the same type twice in a row. The Fox Sparrow's song is composed of loud whistled notes often followed by a buzz or other harsh note. The whistles are very melodic and songs may sound quite beautiful, even though each male typically has just one primary pattern that he varies in length. Referring to the Fox Sparrow, Burroughs remarked in his journal: "Of all the sparrow songs this is the finest."

*Song Sparrow*

The White-throated Sparrow, a north woods species, sings a unique song composed of clear, pure whistles that change in pitch near the song's beginning. Most songs end with triplet notes. The cadence of a common pattern is revealed by two popular memory phrases: *My Sweet, Canada, Canada, Canada*, and *Old Sam Peabody, Peabody, Peabody*. F. Schuyler Mathews, in *Familiar Features of the Roadside* (1897), described the white-throat's song as "remarkable for its high pitch, clear piccolo quality of tone, and freedom from the faintest trace of shrillness." Burroughs, nonetheless, was not impressed, complaining that its song "disappoints one . . . as it ends when it seems only to have begun. If the bird could give us a finishing strain of which this seems only the prelude, it would stand first among feathered songsters."

Although each male white-throat sings only one song pattern, a beautiful concert results when several males occupy one's surroundings, all singing on different pitches. A. West pays tribute to the species in his poem "Northern Nightingale":

> Hark! 'tis our Northern Nightingale that sings
> In far-off, leafy cloisters, dark and cool,
> Fling his flute-notes bounding from the skies!
>
> Thou wild musician of the mountain-streams,
> Most tuneful musician of the forest-choirs,
> Bird of all grace and harmony of soul,
> Unseen, we hail thee for thy blissful voice.

Related to the sparrows are the finches, and several fine singers stand out among them. Both the House Finch and the Purple Finch have delightful melodies, often described as rapid and lively warbles. The House Finch is a common inhabitant of suburbs and cities — its sweet and cheerful outburst adds musical color to stark avenues of concrete and brick. Burroughs considered the Purple Finch one of the leading songsters of the forest choir, remarking in *Wake Robin* (1871) that "His song approaches an ecstasy, and, with the exception of the winter-wren, is the most rapid and copious strain to be heard in these woods."

The Purple Finch's normal song is a short warble, lasting a second or two. However, the species sometimes sings extended songs. Thoreau (May 24, 1855) heard one "sing more than one minute without pause, loud and rich, on an elm tree over the street." Howard Elmore Parkhurst sings praise to the Purple Finch's song in *The Bird's Calendar* (1894): "Of all the more pretentious bird-songs I have ever listened to, that of the purple finch seems the most virile, gladsome, and melodious: as gushing as that of the goldfinch, but less sentimental; vigorous and

*White-throated Sparrow*

not satiating; not formless in modulation, but with a piquant rhythmic phrase, a tripping measure that instantly catches the ear and stirs the blood, a genuine and delightful 'invitation to the dance.' "

*Purple Finch*

Wonderful singers are also found in the Mockingbird family, including the well-known Northern Mockingbird, the Gray Catbird, and a variety of thrashers. The mockingbird is a loud and energetic songster, singing both day and night during the breeding season. Song in this species is actually a long sequence of different songs given with scarcely a pause between them. Some are melodic, some are harsh, and many are imitations of other sounds, especially the songs and calls of birds found in the mockingbird's surroundings. Typically, each song type is repeated three or more times in rapid succession before the male pauses for a fraction of a second and then switches to a new song. Males generally have a hundred or more different song types in their repertoires, and they are always adding new ones.

Given the mockingbird's awesome repertoire, including all the imitations, it is not surprising that it has received attention. However, it is generally not praised for any serene or exalted qualities (as are the thrushes), but rather for the sheer loudness and diversity of its performance. Mark Catesby, a pioneering American naturalist, noted that "The Indians, by way of eminence or imagination, call it *cencontlatoly,* or *four hundred tongues"* (1731). The mocker's knack for imitation is celebrated in Frank L. Stanton's poem, "The Mockingbird" (1894):

> *There come a sound o' melody*
> *No mortal ever heard*
> *An' all the birds seemed singin'*
> *From the throat o' one sweet bird!*

The catbird and the thrashers are relatives of the mockingbird, and all integrate imitations into their songs, to one degree or another. The Brown Thrasher sings a long-continued series of different songs or phrases, normally repeating each twice before moving on to another. This species has far fewer imitations in its repertoire than the mockingbird or the catbird. However, recent research into repertoire size shows that Brown Thrashers may have more than two thousand different song types — perhaps more than any other songbird.

*Northern Mockingbird*

The Gray Catbird also sings a long series of different songs, but he sings each only once, rather than repeating phrases like the Northern Mockingbird and Brown Thrasher. Many songs are squeaky, but some have a pretty, whistled quality, and imitations are common. Each male has a hundred or more different songs in his repertoire. Although capable of producing pleasing notes, the catbird is generally not praised for its melodies. In fact, one anonymous author wondered why a catbird, "gifted with the charm of song," must "do the generous gift such wrong?" In spite of all the squeaky notes, Clinton Scollard, in his poem "A Rain Song," celebrated the catbird's strain:

*Gray Catbird*

*After long days of golden glare,*
*How sweet the music of the rain!*
*And how ecstatic on the air*
*The Catbird's silvery strain!*

A variety of other well-known species have lovely songs. These include the Eastern and Western Meadowlarks, the Bobolink, and backyard favorites such as the American Robin, Northern Cardinal, and Baltimore Oriole.

The song of the Eastern Meadowlark, often delivered from a roadside fence post, consists of plaintive, down-slurred whistles with a tempo sounding like *spring-of-the-year*. The whistles are usually quite musical. Each male has fifty to a hundred or more songs in his repertoire and sings one type a dozen times or so before changing to another. To those living next to fields and meadows, the meadowlark's sweet slurs are a favorite sign of spring.

To many listeners, the song of the Western Meadowlark is more musical than that of its eastern relative. Songs begin with several pure whistles followed by a cascade of gurgling notes that drop in pitch at the end. Each male has five to ten songs in his repertoire and sings one type for a while before switching to another. The song of the Western Meadowlark enlivens grasslands throughout the West; it is one of the loudest, most common, and prettiest songs heard in the region.

*Western Meadowlark*

*Eastern Meadowlark*

*Why I'd give more for one live Bobolink*
*than a square mile o' larks in printer's ink!*
— JAMES RUSSELL LOWELL

*Bobolink*

Another grassland bird, the Bobolink of northern hayfields, is one of our most gifted songsters. Although each male sings just two different song types, these songs are extraordinary outbursts of metallic, gurgling notes delivered while perched or in flight, and sometimes lasting four seconds or more. Songs may even be combined to form compound songs lasting ten seconds or more.

The bubbling, ecstatic quality of the Bobolink's song has been excitedly described by nearly every naturalist who has heard it. F. Schuyler Mathews (1904) called it "a mad, reckless song-fantasia, an outbreak of pent-up, irrepressible glee. The difficulty in either describing or putting upon paper such music is insurmountable." William Cullen Bryant, in his classic poem "Robert of Lincoln" (1893), rendered the song as *Bob-o'-link, bob-o'-link, spink, spank, spink,* but these words fail to convey the extraordinary complexity of the song. Arthur Cleveland Bent called the Bobolink's song "a bubbling delirium of ecstatic music that flows from the gifted throat of the bird like sparkling champagne . . . even the famed mockingbird cannot reproduce it." Thoreau (June 1, 1857) also responded with enthusiasm: "It is as if he touched his harp within a vase of liquid melody, and when he lifted it out, the notes fell like bubbles from the trembling strings." It seems that one cannot truly appreciate the ecstatic wildness of the Bobolink's song until one beholds the bird fluttering above a green grassy meadow, shaking out a flood of delirious, rapturous music for all the world to hear.

No discussion of fine singers is complete without mention of several common neighborhood birds that thrill our ears with music each spring and early summer. The American Robin is perhaps the most familiar songbird in North America, and

*The robin warbled forth his full clear note*
*For hours, and wearied not.*
— William Cullen Bryant

*American Robin*

*Gray Catbird*

*Rose-breasted Grosbeak (immature male)*

its rollicking whistled song, often heard at the break of dawn, offers a refreshing prelude to the coming day. Wilson Flagg (1881) declared that "The Robin is the Philomel of morning twilight . . . He is the chief performer in the delightful anthem that welcomes the rising day." The robin's typical song is composed of several wavering, whistled phrases sounding like *cheerily, cheerio, cheeriup, cheerily,* with short pauses between songs. At dawn, robins often sing a more continuous and spirited version.

Of all our native birds, the robin and its melody are most closely associated with the habitations of man. For Clarence Hawkes, author of *Tenants of the Trees* (1907), the robin's song symbolized childhood security: "One of the first external things that flooded my consciousness, thrilling the awakening soul with new joy, was the song of the robin, filling my little chamber with sweet melody, and causing the child in the crib to lie very still lest the minstrel be frightened away." James Russell Lowell, in his poem "To a Dandelion" (1848), associated the robin's song with the safety and security of his youth, "when birds and flowers and I were happy peers." Thoreau (April 21, 1852) observed the same, but wondered, " 'Did he sing thus in Indian days?' I ask myself; for I have always associated the sound with the village and the clearing, but now I do detect the aboriginal wildness in his strain, and can imagine him a woodland bird, and that he sang thus when there was no civilized ear to hear him, a pure forest melody even like the wood thrush."

The robin is a favorite herald of spring, and to many its song symbolizes the end of winter. Burroughs (1871) celebrated hearing his first robin of the year: "How round and genuine the notes are, and how early our ears drink them in! The first utterance, and the spell of winter is thoroughly broken, and the remembrance of it afar off." Hundreds of poems have been written that convey this sentiment. One of my favorites is "Seeking the May-Flower" (1860) by Edmund Clarence Stedman:

> *The sweetest sound our whole year round —*
> *'Tis the first robin of the spring!*
> *The song of the full orchard choir*
> *Is not so fine a thing.*

Anyone attempting to learn bird songs faces the challenge of distinguishing the robin's song from those of other birds with similar songs. These include the Rose-breasted Grosbeak, Black-headed Grosbeak, Scarlet Tanager, Summer Tanager, and Western Tanager. To many listeners, the songs of the grosbeaks seem richer and brighter than the robin's, clearly superior in musical quality, like a "robin who took singing lessons." The tanagers, on the other hand, have hoarse, burry notes interspersed in their songs, making them sound like a "robin with a sore throat."

*American Robin*

Of the species with robinlike songs, the Rose-breasted Grosbeak perhaps deserves the highest marks. Its song is a delightful ramble of bright, whistled notes, lasting up to four seconds or more. Each male sings a variety of slightly different patterns, some having very pretty endings that give the listener a pleasing sense of musical closure. Leander S. Keyser, author of *In Bird Land* (1897) trumpeted the rose-breasted's superior strain: "At first you may be disposed to think the grosbeak's song much like the robin's, but you will soon find that it is finer in several respects, the tones being clearer and fuller, the utterance more rapid and varied, and the whole song much more spirited; and that is saying a good deal, considering the Cock Robin's cheery carols."

Another favorite backyard bird with a loud whistled song is the Northern Cardinal. The cardinal's bright, slurred whistles complement the brightness of its plumage, making this colorful singer hard to miss as it broadcasts loud songs from the top of a neighborhood oak or maple. The notes making up songs are usually quite musical, and humans can sometimes do convincing whistled imitations.

*Scarlet Tanager*

Typically, a male's song has one or two parts, each composed of repeated whistles. One common pattern sounds something like *purdy, purdy, purdy,—whoit-whoit-whoit-whoit.* Cardinals may also repeat just one whistled phrase, producing songs sounding like *wheet-wheet-wheet-wheet.* Each male has several phrases to draw on and may combine them into ten or more different song patterns. A male often repeats one song pattern for several minutes or more before flying to a new perch and beginning a new song.

Howard Elmore Parkhurst (1894) was not impressed by one cardinal's minimalist effort: "The cardinal's song is especially disappointing, for there are such possibilities in the full, rich tone that do not begin to be realized. Commencing with a clear and magnificent whistle, several times repeated, like a preliminary flourish, you are on the *qui vive* for a glorious performance—and there he stops! Either the mind or the heart (or both) is lacking to say anything more." Although the cardinal's performance is rather simple, one cannot help but congratulate him for singing his few notes so well.

Another neighborhood singer with a rich, whistled song is the colorful Baltimore Oriole. His tone more closely approximates a human whistle than that of any other backyard bird. The oriole ranks low in terms of repertoire size and variation, each male usually singing one primary song type which he may vary in length. Neighboring males, however, usually have very different-sounding songs, making it easy to identify individuals by their songs. Many poets and naturalists have celebrated the oriole's musical whistles. James Russell Lowell (1848) wrote of an

*Northern Cardinal*

*Rose-breasted Grosbeak*

oriole "cheering his labor with a note, rich as the orange of his throat," and John Proctor Mills lauds the bird's bright melody:

> There's a song on each swinging bough —
> Of the forest green with spring,
> There's a golden note from the Oriole's throat —
> That the whisp'ring zephyrs bring.

So, there we have it, a brief survey of some of the finest avian singers in North America — and on the entire earth, for that matter. All these birds have been appreciated since antiquity for their superior musical abilities. They have excited our minds, stirred our emotions, and elevated us spiritually. They probably helped stimulate the creation and development of our own human melodies. Burroughs considered them "the original type and teacher of the poet," noting that we "demand from the human lark or thrush that he 'shake out his carols' in the same free and spontaneous manner as his winged prototypes." While human music has evolved into a plethora of expressions, some feel that nature's original melodies — especially bird songs — are superior in effect. When Burroughs listened to the song of a Hermit Thrush, he experienced a "serene exaltation of sentiment of which music, literature and religion are but faint types and symbols." Who is not moved by the beautiful songs of the birds, and who is not softened by their sacred beauty?

> Teach us, sprite or bird,
> What sweet thoughts are thine:
> I have never heard
> Praise of love or wine
> That panted forth a rapture so divine.
> — PERCY BYSSHE SHELLEY

*Baltimore Oriole (both photos)*

# Lesser Musicians

*While we appreciate the finest singers for the musicality of their songs, they are in the minority when it comes to bird song as a whole. Most bird species have simple, rather mundane songs, often containing harsh and discordant elements. Without doubt, the abundance of nonmusical songs in our surroundings helps accentuate our enjoyment of the finer songs by providing a backdrop for comparison, but these lesser songs can also be appreciated in their own right. Is not each bird satisfied with its own performance? Do not the songs of all birds contribute equally to nature's choir? And if we listen without judgment, are we not able to find beauty and delight in every song we hear?*

Beauty is in the mind of the beholder. If one listens with sensitivity, one can be moved by the most nonmusical of songs. Wilson Flagg observed: "The ignorant and rude are dazzled and delighted by the display of gorgeous splendor, and charmed by loud and stirring sounds. But the more simple melodies and less attractive colors and forms, that appeal to the imagination for their principal effect, are felt only by individuals of a poetic temperament." Samuel Harper encourages us to act like the poets, "for those whose hearts listen when they are in the fields or woods, no bird will rise to its perch without being seen and enjoyed, and no bird will utter its call or sing its song, however soft or ventriloquous, without being heard and loved."

Learning to appreciate the abundance of "lesser singers," if it is appropriate to label them as such, is undoubtedly a matter of education and attitude. Harper (1917) clarifies this point: "Bird notes, with some exceptions, are elusive and indefinite, a part of the composite hum and atmosphere of the woods, and to the careless and unsympathetic ear are not naturally or easily detected and detached from the general ensemble of woods sounds. But to him who is 'fellow to leaf and flower, brook, bee, and bird,' all the little voices of woods and fields 'speak a various language.' " If we embrace this language with a careful and sympathetic ear, we nurture an appreciation for every bird sound we hear, no matter how simple and nonmusical it may be.

We will begin our survey of lesser songsters with a small brown meadow sparrow whose song Roger Tory Peterson (1939) described as "the poorest vocal effort of any bird." The high-pitched, insectlike *tsi-lick* of the male Henslow's Sparrow scarcely sounds like a song, but it does function as song in the life of the bird. One bird biologist took exception to Peterson's

*It is with birds as with other poets:*
*The smaller gift need not be the less genuine.*
— BRADFORD TORREY

remarks, stating that the song of the Henslow's becomes much prettier when played at one-half or one-quarter speed, thus revealing more note complexity and tonal beauty than we normally hear. This is meaningful because it is thought that song-birds are better able than humans to discriminate the intricate details of rapidly delivered high-pitched sounds. In other words, the birds themselves may very well detect aspects of bird songs that escape our human ears.

Poets, of course, hear with a poet's ear, not with a bird's ear. The poets are nonetheless moved by the the Henslow's Sparrow and other sparrows with similar songs. Thoreau (June 14, 1851) imagined a connection with the insect world: "In Conant's orchard I hear the faint cricket-like song of a sparrow saying its vespers, as if it were a link between the cricket and the bird." I personally applaud the Henslow's Sparrow for practicing the law of parsimony. The humble sparrow accomplishes his goal with the least fuss. By singing simply, he impresses me more!

Other native sparrows with insectlike songs include the Grasshopper, Savannah, Sharp-tailed, Le Conte's, and Clay-colored sparrows. Their buzzy songs are difficult for the novice to tell apart, but those who know these birds delight in their notes. Most anyone can appreciate an obviously beautiful bird song, but it takes a measure of refinement to be excited by nonmusical songs such as these.

The sparrows exhibit the full gamut of singing abilities, with many species falling somewhere in the center and often being celebrated for some particular aspect of their song. Two examples are the Field Sparrow and the Black-chinned Sparrow, whose songs are a series of melodic down-slurs that speed up from beginning to end. The songs of these species are two of the finest examples in the bird

*Grasshopper Sparrow*

*Savannah Sparrow*

*A bubble of music floats*
*The slope of the hillside over;*
*A little wandering sparrow's notes;*
*And the bloom of yarrow and clover.*
— LUCY LARCOM

*Field Sparrow*

world of musical *accelerando.* Edward Forbush (1929) provided a nice description of the Field Sparrow's song: "A pensive strain, often varied; usually begins with a few slow, high, clear, prolonged slurred notes, then accelerates, and finally trails off *diminuendo* in rapid repetitions, fading as it ends."

The Flycatcher family is a group characterized by simple nonmusical songs. A familiar backyard species is the Eastern Phoebe, a small gray-brown bird with a buzzy song that sounds much like its name: *fee-beee . . . fee-beee . . . fee-beee . . .* Listening closely, one realizes that the Phoebe actually has two song types that are roughly alternated — one is the burry *fee-beee,* and the other a more sputtering *fi-brreet.* James Russell Lowell (1848)composed a clever poem to describe the Phoebe's humble performance, but he did not distinguish the two song types:

*Eastern Phoebe*

> *Phoebe! is all it has to say*
> *In plaintive cadence o'er and o'er,*
> *Like children that have lost their way,*
> *And know their names, and nothing more.*

A subgroup of flycatchers with simple, rather nonmusical songs includes the members of the genus Empidonax, which includes the Least, Acadian, Willow, and Alder Flycatchers. As every aspiring birder soon discovers, these species look very much alike and are best identified by their songs, which are distinct, but which challenge the listener. The Least sings a dry *che-bek',* the Acadian an emphatic *peet-sa,* the Willow a sneezy *fitz-bew,* and the Alder a buzzy *wee-bé-o.* Once these songs become familiar, the empid flycatchers become a joyful exercise in aural discrimination, albeit not of a musical sort.

Although most flycatchers have non-melodic songs, a notable exception is the Eastern Wood-Pewee, with its plaintive whistled song that stands out amid the other sounds of the forest. The pewee has two primary song types, one a thin wavering whistle, *pee-a-wee,* and the other a down-slurred *peee-oh* (a third song type

*Alder Flycatcher*

occurs during the pewee's special twilight performance, described in the next chapter). Typically, the male sings its *pee-a-wee* song several times in succession, with long pauses between each song, and then finally utters a single *peee-oh* phrase, which imparts a sense of musical closure to the human ear. John Townsend Trowbridge (1903) captures the essence in his poem "The Pewee," where he transcribes the down-slurred song type as *peer:*

*I . . . sat me down*
*Beside the brook, irresolute,*
*And watched a little bird in suit*
*Of sombre olive, soft and brown,*
*Perched in the maple branches, mute . . .*
*"Dear bird," I said, "what is thy name?"*
*And thrice the mournful answer came,*
*So faint and far and yet so near, —*
*"Pe-wee! pe-wee! peer!"*

*Eastern Wood-Pewee*

A host of common neighborhood birds have what we might call lesser songs. For example, consider the Tufted Titmouse, whose repeated *peter-peter-peter* or *peeyer-peeyer-peeyer* sounds like a simplified version of the Carolina Wren's song or a half-hearted effort from a Northern Cardinal. Yet the titmouse's song is definitely musical, and it brightens the neighborhood soundscape from late winter to early summer. A related species, the Black-capped Chickadee, is known more for its dissonant call, *chick-a-dee-dee-dee,* than its melodic whistled song, *hey-sweetie,* which consists of two thin whistles that drop slightly in pitch (the second whistle is actually a slurred doublet). Interestingly, the early poets and naturalists had little to say about the chickadee's whistled song, although Thoreau (March 21, 1858) identified it as a "note with which to welcome the spring" and Emerson referred to it as *"Phe-be . . . thy call in spring."* In his poem "The Titmouse" (1867), Emerson instead focuses on the chickadee's call:

*When piped a tiny voice hard by,*
*Gay and polite, a cheerful cry,*
*"Chic-Chic-a-dee-dee!" saucy note*
*Out of sound heart and merry throat,*
*As if it said, "Good-day, good Sir!*
*Fine afternoon, old passenger!*
*Happy to meet you in these places*
*Where January brings few faces."*

*Black-capped Chickadee*

Black-capped Chickadee

There is no sorrow in thy song, no winter in thy year.
— RALPH WALDO EMERSON

The White-breasted Nuthatch is well known for its nasal *yank-yank* calls, but it also has a melodic song that often passes unnoticed — a rapid series of pleasant, albeit somewhat nasal, notes sounding like a laughing *hee-hee-hee-hee-hee-hee*. This is perhaps the first song heard in the new year, emanating from woodlots on warm days from midwinter on, sometimes as early as December or January. Thoreau (March 5, 1859) thought it sounded "more like a song" than any other nuthatch sound, and noted that it is heard "fabulously early in the season, when we men had just begun to anticipate the spring." He once mistook it for the distant tapping of a woodpecker, remarking lyrically: "When only the snow had begun to melt and no rill of song had broken loose, a note so dry and fettered still, so inarticulate and half thawed out, that you might (and would commonly) mistake [it] for the tapping of a woodpecker."

The House Wren is the most common and widespread wren in North America. A familiar denizen of yard and garden, its exuberant, bubbling song is given with head up and tail up, throat feathers expanded and vibrating, body shaking all the while. Burroughs (1871) knew of "no other bird that so throbs and palpitates with

*White-breasted Nuthatch*

*House Wren*

*Blue Jay*

music as this little vagabond." Longfellow may have been describing a House Wren when he wrote "from a neighboring thicket the wildest of singers, swinging aloft on a willow spray that hung over the water, shook from his little throat such floods of delerious music that the whole air and woods and waves seemed silent to listen." The American Indians were also impressed by the House Wren's excited song — the Chippewas named the bird *O-du-na'-mis-sug-ud-da-we'-shi,* meaning "a big noise for its size" (Cooke, 1884).

Among the most vocal of our common birds are members of the family Corvidae, which includes the Blue Jay, American Crow, Fish Crow, and Common Raven. All these species make a lot of noise, but none possesses a true song, at least as we normally define it. The Blue Jay's most typical sound is a discordant *djay,* a raucous call subject to much variation in timing and quality. Thoreau (February 12, 1854), hearing the call on a cold winter day, described it vividly: "You hear . . . the unrelenting steel-cold scream of a jay, ummelted, that never flows into song, a sort of wintry trumpet, screaming cold; hard, tense, frozen music, like the winter sky itself." Eben Pearson Dorr, noting the apparent lack of song, criticized the jay with a poem:

> *The Jay he sings a scanty lay,*
> *As boy who would a fiddle play,*
> *Strikes one bar from tuneful harp,*
> *Then screeches into discord sharp.*
> *Though boys to task again can turn,*
> *The bird, alas! may never learn.*
>
> *Creator placed within his throat*
> *A song that is a single note.*
> *Yet sweet this mellow minor chord,*
> *Prelude, perhaps it pleased the Lord*
> *To song reserved for other shore,*
> *Now vaguely hinted — nothing more.*

Actually, Blue Jays are capable of producing an extraordinary range of sounds, as Ernest Thompson Seton noted in *Bird Portraits* (1901): "Besides the ordinary *djay, djay,* the loud scream so familiar in the autumn woods, the Jay has other cries; a note like a wheelbarrow turning on an ungreased axle, a high scream exactly like the Red-shouldered Hawk's, and such a variety of lesser notes that one never is surprised to find that any unusual sound heard in the woods is produced by the Blue Jay."

American Crows also make a variety of sounds. The common call is a throaty *caw* or *cah,* given with so many variations and in so many situations that we might surmise that an entire "crow language" is built around this single motif. Bradford Torrey was impressed by the social quality of crow talk: "The cawing of a dozen or two of crows, who were talking politics among the pines on the

*Fish Crow*

New Hampshire hillside, affected me most agreeably. There was something of a real neighborliness about it. I would gladly have taken hand in the discussion, if they would have let me." Crows make other sounds as well, including an odd sputtering outburst and soft piping notes heard only at close range. Although crows lack song as it is normally defined, pairs sometimes exchange a rambling series of soft, intimate calls that may have songlike functions.

Of all backyard bird sounds, perhaps the least musical is the song of the Common Grackle, a blackbird recognized by its long tail and iridescent plumage. The male's song, given as he leans forward, puffs out his feathers, and cocks his wings, sounds like a raspy squeak. Groups of courting grackles often gather in evergreens or other trees, with males performing their song displays in front of eager females. Clarence Hawkes (1907) described such a group: "I heard a great commotion in an old elm near the house. It was not a song, although there were many voices, but the noisiest medley of squeaks, squawks, pipes, whistles, and other sounds too queer to have a name. All the tones were wheezy, and some sounded petulant and scolding." To commemorate his experience, Hawkes penned a wonderful little poem:

> *The Grackles are here and that is quite clear.*
> *The morning is ringing,—not with their singing,*
> *But with their talking, they're piping and squawking*
> *Some scandalous ditty, the more then's the pity.*
> *The Grackles are here, that's plain to your ear . . .*

*Common Grackle (above and right)*

The Red-winged Blackbird, a relative of the grackle that breeds in meadows and marshes, has one of the prettiest songs in the blackbird group. It is as if the red-wing took a squeak and transformed it into a melody — a bubbly *o-ka-leee* or *conk-la-reee,* one of the familiar sounds of spring. Like the grackle, the red-wing leans forward and spreads his wings as he sings, exposing bright red shoulder patches. Thoreau (April 22, 1852) decribed his song as "liquid, bubbling, watery, almost like a tinkling fountain," adding that "it oozes, trickles, tinkles, bubbles from his throat, — *bob-y-lee-e-e."* In his poem "May-Day" (1867), Emerson conveyed the essence of the red-wing's performance with a simple sprinkling of words: "The red-wing flutes his *o ka lee."*

Lesser singers abound and we could go on and on describing them, but these examples should suffice to stimulate your interest. However, my review would not be complete without mentioning a forest songster that has gained notoriety for the sheer persistence of its singing — the Red-eyed Vireo, a small olive-colored bird of the treetops. Although rarely seen, the red-eyed makes itself known by singing high-pitched, robinlike songs all day long, with little interruption, from May until August. *High up, treetop, here I am, way up, see me, look up, treetop . . . ,* the male seems to say with high, wavering whistles, repeated almost endlessly with scarcely a pause. Surprisingly, each male has around fifty different songs, though many sound alike to the human ear. One biologist followed a male Red-eyed Vireo for an entire day during the breeding season and found that it "spent nearly ten hours singing a total of 22,197 songs!"

*Red-winged Blackbird (left), Red-eyed Vireo (above)*

The red-eyed's monotonous repetition of similar-sounding songs has earned it the nickname "preacher-bird." William Hamilton Gibson (1891), listening to a red-eyed singing in the forest, described his impression: "It is the voice of the 'preacher' celebrating his matins in his temple of the tree-top, and filling the morning with unremitting praise and counsel — the most sustained and tireless song, and the most communicative voice among all our birds. Often I have sat by the hour beneath his shrine, and long is the list of mellifluous exclamations, exhortations, text, and precepts which I have caught from his [noisy] throat." Alice Ball (1916) gives a rhyming voice to the bird in her poem celebrating its song:

> *Do you hear me? Don't you know*
> *I'm the Red-eyed Vireo?*
> *After lovely blossoming May*
> *Entices me the livelong day —*
> *Even when the August noon*
> *Silences the bards of June —*
> *My incessant voice is heard*
> *Till I'm called The Preacher-Bird.*

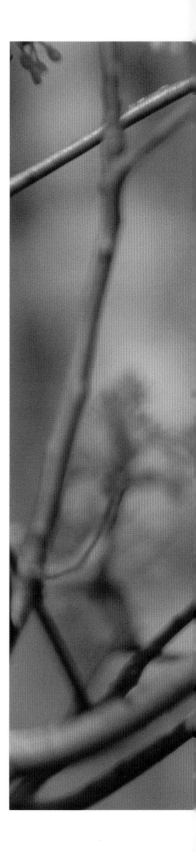

Surveying the entire cast of birds in nature's choir, it becomes clear that only a small percentage have songs that are exceptional by human musical standards. But we must remember that birds do not sing according to our standards — their music is their own, an expression of forces largely outside the human realm. Although we may place certain species in a "lesser musician" category, perhaps we should not belittle their performances. Instead, we can accept and embrace their songs without judgment, for all contribute equally to the choir. As Henry Van Dyke so rightly expressed, "the woods would be very silent if no birds sang there except those that sang best." If we learn to listen with an open, accepting attitude, we will find that all bird songs are a delight to our ears, including the most dissonant and least musical of the lot. In the words of one enlightened naturalist:

> *It is with birds as with other poets: the smaller gift need not*
> *be the less genuine; and they whom the world calls great . . .*
> *may possibly not be the ones who touch us most intimately,*
> *or to whom we return oftenest and with most delight.*
> — BRADFORD TORREY

*Red-eyed Vireo*

# Flight Songs and Night Songs

*When we learn to identify bird songs in the field, we first familiarize ourselves with the typical songs of each species, the normal singing patterns that we hear time and again. However, once we have learned commonplace patterns, we are often surprised when a familiar bird suddenly treats us to a new performance, singing in a totally new way, often under unique circumstances. These atypical, special songs add spice to our listening experience. To the veteran listener, they stand out against the background of normal singing like a shooting star stands out against the night sky. What are these special peformances? How do we recognize them when they occur? And what meaning do they have in the lives of the birds?*

Thoreau and Emerson were both mystified by the striking aerial performance of a "night-warbler" they had trouble identifying. As Thoreau described it on May 18, 1860, the mystery bird, usually in the twilight of dusk, "launches into air above the forest, or over some hollow or open space in the woods, and challenges the attention of the woods by its rapid and impetuous warble, and then drops down swiftly into the tree-tops like a performer withdrawing behind the scenes, and he is very lucky who detects where it alights."

Thoreau was describing the flight song of the Ovenbird, a common forest warbler whose normal song is a loud, ringing *teacher, teacher, teacher, teacher*. For reasons that elude biologists, the Ovenbird and various other species in the warbler family periodically fly into the air and pour forth a song pattern clearly different from the one normally given from a perch. The Ovenbird flight song begins with several high-pitched chips as the male ascends from branch to branch in the forest. When he finally launches into the air above the tree crowns, he begins with several typical *teacher-teacher* phrases, followed by an outburst of complex warbling that Burroughs (1871) described as an "ecstasy of song—clear, ringing, copious, . . . one of the rarest bits of bird-melody to be heard, . . . often indulged in late afternoon or after sundown." On moonlit nights, the male Ovenbird may repeat his "ecstasy song" time and again, showering the night sky with his glittering stardust warble.

*I hear the night-warbler*
*breaking out as in his dreams . . .*
    — HENRY DAVID THOREAU

A number of other warblers have special flight songs, most notably the Common Yellowthroat, Yellow-breasted Chat, Mourning Warbler, Canada Warbler, Nashville Warbler, and our native waterthrushes. The Common Yellowthroat's performance is similar to the Ovenbird's, but is given only during the daytime in the yellowthroat's brushy habitats. It begins with a series of high-pitched chips as the bird flies into the air, followed by a warbling jumble that includes some of the yellowthroat's typical *witchety-witchety* song phrases. Its likeness to the Ovenbird's flight song was clearly a source of confusion for Thoreau (August 5, 1858): "Fair Haven Pond. While passing there, I heard what I should call my night warbler's note, and, looking up, saw the bird dropping to a bush on the hillside. Looking through the glass, I saw that it was the Maryland yellow-throat!! and it afterward flew to the button-bushes in the meadow."

*Canada Warbler*

Warblers are not the only songbirds with flight songs. Many sparrows and finches sing in flight, including the Vesper Sparrow, Seaside Sparrow, and Indigo Bunting. In most of these species, the flight song is an extended or excited version of normal song, or else a more elaborate outburst that includes some typical song phrases. In addition, flight songs are often given as the singer hovers above his territory or flies slowly in a fluttering, butterfly-like manner. In most cases where scientists have studied flight songs, they have not been able to clearly explain their purpose. Are these special flight performances given to attract mates, repel neighboring males, or draw predators from the nest? Or do they represent some other complex motivational state that eludes definition? As one scientist concluded after studying the Ovenbird flight song, "It seems impossible to assess the communicatory value of the flight song, regardless of how dramatic it is. Its rare occurrence and peculiar situation of use, plus the obvious influence of low light level on its elicitation, make it difficult to suggest its function."

Our two native meadowlarks also exhibit special flight songs that contrast sharply with their typical perch songs. The rarely heard flight song of the Eastern Meadowlark is apparently sung only during intense aggressive interactions between males. Arthur Allen described it in his *Book of Bird Life* (1930): "Ordinarily, the Meadowlark sings from a fence-post or the top of a tree in the open, but, occasionally, in a burst of enthusiasm, he mounts upward in the air on quivering wings and repeats and modulates his song until it is scarcely recognizable." In contrast, the Western

*Western Meadowlark*

*Once more the song birds set the air athrill*
*With symphonies of praise,*
*And birds and blossoms grow to music's trill*
*In warm and sheltered ways.*
— BENJAMIN LEGGETT

*Indigo Bunting*

Meadowlark's flight song is commonly heard. It begins with sweet, plaintive whistles that accelerate into a jumble of squeaky, metallic notes that bear little resemblance to the melodic whistles that typify normal perch songs. A relative of the meadowlarks, the Bobolink also sings in flight, its flight song being "a grand medley of warbles and banjo-like notes that can be confused with nothing else" (Allen, 1930).

Perhaps the most famous of all songbird flight displays is the aerial performance of the Skylark of Europe, the inspiration for Percy Bysshe Shelley's famous poem "To a Skylark" (1820), from which the following verse is drawn:

*Bobolink*

> *Higher still and higher*
> *From the earth thou springest*
> *Like a cloud of fire;*
> *The blue deep thou wingest,*
> *And singing still dost soar, and soaring ever singest.*

Shelley was deeply moved by the Skylark's flight display, in which the tiny bird spirals upward above its territory, all the while singing high-pitched bubbling trills and other notes. Heard by itself, the Skylark's song is not particularly impressive, but in its natural context it has a profound effect on those with a poetic ear. Even Shakespeare was impressed: "Hark, hark, the lark at heaven's gate sings" (*Cymbeline*, Act 2, circa 1610). And Thomas Gray praised the performance in his "Ode on the Pleasure Arising from Vicissitude" (circa 1754): "the skylark warbles high, his trembling, thrilling ecstasy; and, lessening from the dazzled sight, melts into air and liquid light."

The Skylark is not native to North America, but the Horned Lark is native here, frequenting barren areas such as sandy beaches, meadows, and prairie. Its song, given from perches or while flying high above its territory, is high-pitched and tinkling, much like the skylark's. Frank Chapman (1897) apparently did not find it beautiful: "The Horned Lark, like its famous relative and many other terrestrial species, sings while on the wing, soaring high above the earth, and often repeating its song many times before alighting. The effort is worthy of better results, for the bird's song is simple and unmusical." Would that Chapman had listened with Shelley's ear! The flight song of the Sprague's Pipit, heard in our northern prairies, rivals the skylark's in effect. Circling above its territory, the male pipit sings beautiful jingling trills that sound like a small chain being dropped into a coil on the ground.

*Horned Lark*

Flight songs such as those of the larks and pipits, given many times during the day, probably function like normal song to attract mates and keep other males away. They may complement ground singing, or else function as the primary or sole mode of singing (especially in grassland habitats where prominent perches are not available). Of course, conjecture about the functions of flight songs does not really touch upon the emotional state of the singing bird. One can scarcely imagine what an Ovenbird or lark might actually feel as it launches upward in ecstasy flight and sings at heaven's gate.

While the Ovenbird sings its flight song at dusk, a number of other songbirds utter their normal daytime songs as the light fades. On page 29 we discussed the evening songs of thrushes and how such songs have an accentuated, magical quality at dusk because most other birds are silent. The same holds true for other dusk singers such as the Field Sparrow and Vesper Sparrow. In fact, both these species have been called "vesper-sparrows" because of their habit of producing evensongs (in reference to the vespers or evening prayers of religious groups such as the Benedictine monks). Burroughs (1871), describing the Field Sparrow, observed that "his song is most noticeable after sundown, when other birds are silent." Thoreau (April 25, 1841) dubbed the Field Sparrow "Nature's minstrel of serene hours," who "sings of an immense leisure and duration."

Pursuing a Vesper Sparrow at dusk, Thoreau (May 12, 1857) wrote: "He sits on some gray perch like himself, on a stake, perchance, in the midst of the field, and you can hardly see him against the plowed ground. You advance step by step as the twilight deepens, and lo! he is gone, and in vain you strain your eyes to see whither, but anon his tinkling strain is heard from some other quarter." Edith Thomas creates a relaxing image in her evensong poem, which could refer to either of the two species:

*Upon a pasture stone,*
*Against the fading west,*
*A small bird sings alone,*
*Then dives and finds a nest.*

*Vesper Sparrow*

*Field Sparrow*

*Northern Mockingbird*

Several native songbirds sing in the middle of the night. One common species well known for this behavior is the Northern Mockingbird (also discussed on page 36), whose nighttime songs often keep people from sleep (it is thought that only unpaired males sing at night). Walt Whitman, in "Out of the Cradle Endlessly Rocking" (1859), praised a mockingbird, who shook out "carols under that lagging, yellow, waning moon." Richard Henry Wilde (1867) thought its moonlight song "a soft, sweet, pensive, solemn strain." Forbush (1929) was also impressed, noting that night-singing mockingbirds may also sing in flight: "On moonlit nights at this season the inspired singer launches himself far into the air, filling the silvery spaces of the night with the exquisite swells and trills, liquid and sweet, of his unparalleled melody. The song rises and falls, as the powers of the singer wax and wane, and so he serenades his mate the live-long night."

Another night-singing species is the Gray Catbird, whose squeaky songs are quite beautiful when heard in the quiet darkness. An anonymous author referred to the catbird's night song as a "liquid-strain" poured out like "music-rain." Among the wrens, the Sedge Wren and Marsh Wren often sing at night from wet meadows and marshes. A variety of sparrows may also be heard at night, including the Henslow's, Sharp-tailed, White-throated, and several other species. Among the warblers, the Yellow-breasted Chat (discussed later in this chapter) often sings at night, either perched or in flight. In all instances, hearing songs against a backdrop of typical night sounds accentuates their aesthetic quality, the songs of most other songbirds being conspicuously absent.

There is a great rush of singing in the twilight of dawn in spring and early summer — bird song is at its height during the hour or two before sunrise. Nearly every species advertises its presence with gusto. However, if one listens carefully, one discovers that a variety of species sing special versions of song during these wee hours, unique song types that may be referred to as "dawn songs" or "twilight songs."

*Gray Catbird*

*Eastern Wood-Pewee*

Perhaps the most famous of these is the twilight song of the Eastern Wood-Pewee, a member of the Flycatcher family. As mentioned on page 52 , the pewee's normal singing involves two plaintive whistled songs: a wavering *pee-a-wee,* usually sung several times in succession with many seconds of silence between, and a down-slurred *peee-oh,* sung less often and rarely repeated twice in a row. At dawn, the pace of singing is faster, with only a second of silence between songs, and a third phrase is added — a rising *ah-di-day* not heard during daytime singing. At the height of the twilight performance, pewees tend to sing the three song types in immediate succession for minutes on end: *pee-a-wee . . . peee-oh . . . ah-di-day . . .* and so on, a sad but beautiful melody set against the brightening sky. This performance may be repeated at dusk, though usually with less vigor.

Other flycatchers have special twilight songs, including the Acadian Flycatcher, Great-crested Flycatcher, and the Eastern and Western Kingbirds. The daytime song of the Acadian Flycatcher is an explosive *peet-sa,* with long periods of silence between songs. At dawn and at dusk, the Acadian sings more continuously, giving voice to several different song phrases separated by short pauses. For the Great-crested Flycatcher and the kingbirds, dawn song is the only song of the species — once the sun is up, these birds quit singing entirely and only give calls.

Many of our native warblers sing special songs at dawn. For instance, the normal daytime song of the Northern Parula is a rising, buzzy *zeeeeeeee-up.* At dawn, the song is a rapid rolling series of notes followed by buzzes and an accented ending. Similarly, the Blue-winged Warbler sings a simple *beeee-bzzzz* throughout the

*When birds sang out their mellow lay,*
*And winds were soft and woods were green,*
*And the song ceased not with the day*
— HENRY WADSWORTH LONGFELLOW

*Northern Parula*

*Sedge Wren*

*Blue-winged Warbler*

*Trills a wild and wondrous note,*
*The sweetest sound that ever stirred*
*A warbler's throat.*
— OLIVE THORNE MILLER

*Black-throated Green Warbler*

day, but gives a more complicated performance at dawn. Another example is the Black-throated Green Warbler, whose normal song is a high-pitched *zee-zee-zee-zoo-zee*. At dawn, this species changes its pattern to a more leisurely *zoo, zee, zoo-zoo, zee*. In the Chesnut-sided Warbler, American Redstart, Yellow Warbler, and many other species, dawn songs sound much like normal songs but have an accented ending that sets them apart.

Scientists have found that warblers sometimes sing their dawn songs during the day, but only during aggressive encounters between males. They hypothesize that these special song types are associated with high levels of aggression in the singer. It is possible that a male, singing at dawn when threats from other males are not evident, is actually sending a powerful message to male competitors: "This territory is occupied and I'm ready to defend it." But, even if this message is embodied in his song, we do not know if the male is aware that he is sending such a message, or that he feels aggressive as he sings peacefully in the twilight.

Certain members of the Sparrow family also have special dawn songs. Most notable is the Field Sparrow, whose normal song is an accelerating series of slurred whistles. At dawn, this sparrow sings complex multipart songs. As with the warblers, the Field Sparrow sings its dawn song during daytime aggressive encounters, suggesting a relationship to aggression. The Chipping Sparrow also has a special dawn performance that is thought to communicate aggression. Its normal song is a long, dry trill lasting several seconds, usually delivered from a perch high in a tree, with pauses of many seconds between songs. At dawn, the male perches on the ground, often near a neighboring male, and delivers shortened songs in a more lively sequence, like short bursts of machine gun fire. Perhaps Thoreau was hearing these bursts when he awoke on June 2, 1853, to "the low universal chirping or twittering of chip-birds . . . bursting . . . on the surface of the uncorked day."

The Eastern Towhee provides an interesting variant on the dawn song pattern. Each male has about five different song types in his repertoire. During the day, he sings one type for an extended period before switching to another, passing through his entire repertoire in about an hour. At dawn, he sings much more energetically, switching song types after every song and going through his entire repertoire in twenty to thirty seconds!

Many other species sing differently at dawn, but their songs have not been studied in detail. For example, the American Robin's excited and continuous twilight song merits further attention. Likewise, the Scarlet Tanager and Summer Tanager seem to have distinct dawn songs, but these are not described in the literature. These species and others await the sharp ears and open minds of scientists and poets alike.

*Chipping Sparrow*

*The robin is the one that interrupts the morn,*
*With hurried, few, express reports,*
*When March is scarcely on.*
　　　　　　　—EMILY DICKINSON

*American Robin*

It is unfortunate that early poets and naturalists did not have access to the scientific knowledge that we have today, for they had such a way with words! Consider, for example, Thoreau's remarkable description of robins singing excitedly at dawn (April 16, 1856): "The robins sing with will now. What a burst of melody! It gurgles out of all conduits now; they are choked with it. There is such a tide and rush of songs as when a river is straightened between two rocky walls. It seems as if morning's throat were not large enough to emit all this sound." Reading his lines, I know in my heart that Thoreau heard what I hear when the robin's twilight melody flows in through my bedroom window, rousing me from sleep and filling the dawn with an exploding rush of cheer.

A variety of songbirds have special song types associated with specific situations or events. For instance, males of many species sing excitedly when their mates solicit copulation. This is true of the House Wren and House Finch. In both cases, the male pursues his receptive mate vigorously, singing song after song without pause, and adding a variety of shrill, high-pitched notes to his performance. The Purple Finch has a unique response to aerial predators. When it spots a hawk, the finch may approach and sing a series of disjointed squeaky phrases reminiscent of the song of a vireo. This is not actually song in a strict sense, although it sounds like song to the human ear. The Grasshopper Sparrow has a remarkably complex song that is very different from its typical insectlike *pi-tup-zeeeeeee.* Periodically during the day, and for no apparent reason, males suddenly shake loose songs that are an extremely rapid stuttering ramble of high-pitched notes. This unusual performance has defied clear scientific explanation, although it may be related to aggressive situations, like the dawn songs mentioned earlier.

*Grasshopper Sparrow*

*Eastern Towhee*

When male songbirds encounter one another near territory boundaries, they often respond by singing back and forth, alternating their songs in a nonrandom and nonoverlapping fashion. This is termed "countersinging," and males of many species practice it. Furthermore, in species in which males have large repertoires, and in which neighboring males share song types, one may observe both countersinging and the matching of song patterns. Such "matched countersinging" can be heard in many species, including common birds such as the Tufted Titmouse, Northern Cardinal, Marsh Wren, and Song Sparrow. Typically, the interacting males exchange the same or very similar song types for several minutes before one suddenly switches to a different type, at which time his adversary follows suit. Scientists surmise that such behavior is equivalent to flinging an insult at one's rival by throwing back its exact same song. In any event, it is a sign of intense interaction.

*Red-winged Blackbird (female)*

Interestingly, some species countersing but avoid song matching. A good example is the Wood Thrush. Each male has a number of song types in his repertoire, and neighbors often have similar songs to draw upon. However, when two thrushes countersing, they usually respond with a song clearly different from the one just heard. As listeners, we are grateful because this results in auditory delight — two thrushes tossing beautiful songs back and forth in close succession, with no two sounding alike! Thoreau caught on to this, remarking on June 22, 1852, "I hear around me, but never in sight, the many wood thrushes whetting their steellike notes. Such keen singers! It takes a fiery heat, many dry pine leaves added to the furnace of the sun, to temper their strains! Always they are either rising or falling to a new strain. After what a moderate pause they deliver themselves again! saying ever a new thing, avoiding repetition, methinks answering one another." Are the two wood thrushes really exchanging insults, or is this a mutual celebration of their extraordindary musical prowess — or both?

Song interactions between mates also occur. In species in which females occasionally sing, such as the Northern Cardinal and Baltimore Oriole, mates exchange songs during pair formation, sometimes in a countersinging fashion. An inexperienced listener might think he's hearing two males singing. In the Black-headed Grosbeak, females sing in the vicinity of the nest, possibly to attract the male to help with incubation. In other species, such as the Red-winged Blackbird, males and females sing very different sounding songs, often in a duetting fashion. Redwing males are sometimes polygynous and may have more than one female on their breeding territories. The females are also territorial, each defending the area around its nest from neighboring females with the help of a sputtering outburst that functions much like male song. In addition, a female often duets with her mate, responding to his song with her sputter.

*Baltimore Oriole (female)*

*Red-winged Blackbird*

Similar duetting occurs among Brown-headed Cowbirds, with the female giving a metallic trill as the male sings his squeaky song. The female Carolina Wren also duets with her mate, blending her harsh chatter with his song, especially during territorial encounters with neighboring pairs. Female Eastern Bluebirds occasionally sing, especially when disturbed around the nest. The female sounds much like the male, and it is thought that she sings to attract her mate to the nest so that he will help defend it.

The Northern Mockingbird was featured on page 36 not only for its varied, melodic song, but also for its striking ability to mimic the sounds of other birds. The mocker's imitations are amazing, especially to a listener familiar with bird sounds. In fact, the mockingbird is a great test of one's knowledge—the more bird sounds you can identify, the more imitations you will hear in a mocker's song.

The mockingbird, catbird, thrasher, and other members of the Mockingbird family are not the only imitators. Another expert is the European Starling, an introduced species. The song of the starling, a remarkable sequence of sounds lasting many seconds, must be heard up close to be appreciated. It begins with a series of whistled notes, which are followed by a number of variable and complex phrases that include cases of mimicry. The sequence finally ends with excited rattles and clicks and loud high-pitched sounds that are hard to imagine being produced by a bird. Leander Keyser (1897) provides an accurate description: "Never before had I listened to such divers sounds from a bird's throat, nor had I even fancied that they were possible . . . He begins in a low, subdued tone, and seems at first to be quite calm; but gradually he grows excited, his body quivers and sways from side to side, his neck is craned out, his throat expands and contracts convulsively, and, oh! oh! oh! — pardon the exclamations — the hurly-burly that gurgles and ripples and bubbles forth from his windpipe! . . . It is simply wonderful."

Another great imitator is our largest native warbler, the Yellow-breasted Chat. The chat's song is an odd assortment of whistles, rattles, squeaks, and other weird sounds delivered at a leisurely pace, often during flight. Commonly included are imitations of birds and other creatures. Burroughs (1871) found the chat impressive, writing, "His voice is . . . quite uncanny . . . in rapid succession follow notes the most discordant that ever broke the sylvan silence. How he barks like a puppy, then quacks like a duck, then rattles like a kingfisher, then squalls like a fox, then caws like a crow, then mews like a cat . . . *C-r-r-r-r-r, — whrr, — that's it, — chee, — quack, cluck, —yit, yit, yit, — now hit it, —t-r-r-r-r, — when, caw, caw, —cut, cut, —tea-boy —who, who, — mew, mew, —*and so on till you are tired of listening." The chat also regularly sings at night, especially during moonlit nights.

*European Starling*

*Yellow-breasted Chat*

Learning bird songs is a never-ending pursuit. Once one learns the typical singing behavior of a species, one often discovers variations that challenge the best of listeners. Some species have complex song repertoires and we get confused when we hear a new theme. Furthermore, the same species may sing somewhat differently depending on geographic location. In addition, individual birds sometimes present us with atypical songs that we do not recognize at first. Learning about all these variations is challenging enough, but the situation gets even more complicated. Many birds treat us to special performances such as flight songs, night songs, dawn songs, and twilight songs. And when we include interactions between individuals, we discover special courtship songs along with instances of countersinging, song matching, song mismatching, and duetting between mates. On top of this, species that mimic the sounds of other birds challenge our ability to distinguish originals from imitations!

Despite these challenges, experiencing and learning the themes and variations of each species' song opens the door to a deeper level of appreciation. The commonplace is easy to learn and enjoy, but it is the less common patterns and the unsolved mysteries that delight us the most. Imagine Thoreau's pleasure each time he heard his mysterious night-warbler "breaking out as in his dreams." Every bird reveals intimate secrets of song to those who wander the forests and fields, listening. You must be willing to admit ignorance, as Bradford Torrey (1885) knew so well: "It is an indiscretion ever to say of a bird that he has only such and such notes. You may have been his friend for years, but the next time you go into the woods he will likely enough put you to shame by singing something not so much as hinted at in your description." Imagine the narrowness of only knowing the Ovenbird's daytime song, when a much greater delight can be experienced at dusk, when the warbler soars above the trees and sings its magical twilight hymn:

> *There are few roamers of the woods who have not often heard a ringing "teacher-teacher-teacher-teacher" echo through their aisle and seen the chorister, the oven bird, walking sedately on a horizontal bough. But, if we remain in the wood till sundown is close at hand, we shall see him soar up through the trees, pouring forth an indescribable, but beautiful song, until the night wraps the woods in shadow and silence.*
>
> — Reginald Heber Howe

*Ovenbird*

# Dawn Chorus

*Rising at dawn in the spring and early summer, we are greeted by an extraordinary abundance of bird song. Nearly every species is in full song, singing more excitedly than normal and often giving special performances tailored for dawn's early light. This twilight chorus is amazing to behold, and one cannot help but think the birds themselves are inspired by it, singing, listening, and partaking in a glorious anthem to the unfolding day. The chorus sometimes overwhelms us — it is truly a challenge to pick out the songs of all the different species. We cannot help but wonder why so much singing occurs at dawn and how individual birds manage to be heard. In the confusion of sound, are different species timing their songs to stand out in the chorus? And why does the dawn chorus fill us with such wonder and delight?*

Poets, naturalists, and scientists alike have been impressed by the heightened activity of singing birds at dawn. Wilson Flagg, in *A Year With the Birds* (1881), perhaps said it best: "Early in the morning, when the purple light of dawn first awakens us from sleep, and while the red rays that fringe the eastern arches of the sky with a beautiful tremulous motion are fast brightening into a more dazzling radiance . . . we are overwhelmed by the vocal and multitudinous chorus of the feathered tribe . . . There is first an occasional twittering, then a single performance from some early waker, then a gradual joining of new voices, until at length there is a full chorus of song. Every few minutes some new voice joins the concert, as if aroused by the beginners and excited by emulations, until thousands of melodious voices seem to be calling us out from sleep."

Why do birds sing so much at dawn? Scientists offer a number of reasons that may help explain the behavior. First, sound transmission is very good at dawn because of reduced air turbulence — dawn is usually the calmest part of the day and therefore is an excellent time for singing. In addition, feeding conditions are poor at dawn. Cool temperatures depress insect activity and low light makes it difficult for birds to see prey. Thus, it seems logical for birds to sing during the twilight period and switch to foraging after sunrise. It is also thought that territorial vacancies are highest at dawn, primarily because of the nocturnal activity of mammalian predators. Males without territories may search for unoccupied areas at dawn. By singing immediately upon waking, a male makes it clear that he has survived the night and that he's

*In the morning . . . we are overwhelmed by the multitudinous chorus of the feathered tribe.*
— WILSON FLAGG

still defending his territory. The existence of special dawn songs in many species, and evidence that such songs are associated with high levels of aggression, support the notion that dawn singing is primarily a male-to-male communication, an aggressive expression of territoriality. However, dawn singing may also be important to females. Early in the season, migrant females may arrive at night and begin looking for a mate at dawn, attracted by the songs of territorial males. Female fertility may also be at a peak in the morning. Once mated, a male often awakens first and sings until his mate emerges from the nest, at which time the pair copulates. Singing may help coordinate this mating activity.

Whatever the reasons, song production is clearly accentuated at dawn. Is the chorus just a random overlapping of the songs of individuals and species, possessing no particular structure of its own? Listeners usually form a different impression. One may perceive pleasing patterns in the chorus, as if the singers are interacting, contributing to something greater than their individual performances. Is it possible that the dawn chorus is not a random thing, but rather the result of complex interactions between individual and species?

Wilson Flagg thought the dawn chorus part of a larger scheme — a creation involving the cooperation of many species, directed by higher natural forces to produce a harmonious anthem: "Nature has so arranged the harmony of this chorus, that one part shall assist another; and so exquisitely has she combined all the different voices, that the silence of any cannot fail to be immediately perceived. The low, mellow warble of the Bluebird seems an echo to the louder voice of the Robin; and the incessant trill or running accompaniment of the Hair-Bird [Chipping Sparrow], the twittering of the Swallow, and the loud, melodious piping of the Oriole, frequent and short, are sounded like different parts of a band of instruments, and each performer seems to time his part as if by some rule of harmony."

Thoreau (July 7, 1852) imagined that the dawn chorus sprang from environmental causes, an alchemical transformation of evaporating mist: "The first really foggy morning. Yet before I rise I hear the song of birds from out it, like the bursting of its bubbles with music, the bead on liquid just uncorked. Their song gilds thus the frothwork of the morning. As if the fog were a great sweet froth on the surface of land and water, whose fixed air escaped, whose bubbles burst with music. The sound of its evaporation, the fixed air of the morning just brought from the cellars of night escaping. The morning twittering of the birds in perfect harmony with it . . . the fog condenses into fountains and streams of music, as into the strain of the bobolink which I heard, and runs off so. The music of the birds is the tinkling of the rills that flow from it."

*Rose-breasted Grosbeak (immature male)*

*Northern Cardinal*

Is there a special harmony in the dawn chorus? Is the chorus an expression of forces other than the selfish adaptive concerns of the individual participants? We do not know for certain, but there is scientific evidence for interactions that produce patterns pleasing to our ears, especially evidence for the tendency of birds to time their singing to avoid competition. We've already mentioned countersinging (page 82), which by itself would lend an element of structure to a chorus. Similarly, in Red-winged Blackbirds, singing males often adopt a leader-follower relationship, with the "follower" male singing immediately after he hears the song of his adversary. But these are examples of interactions between individuals of a single species. Is there evidence of similar interactions between different species? The answer is yes. In a recent study of Red-eyed Vireos and Least Flycatchers, researchers found that a flycatcher will avoid singing while a vireo is singing (although vireos do not seem to respond likewise to the songs of flycatchers). Another study of several forest species showed that Ovenbirds avoid overlapping their songs with the songs of other species, thus reducing auditory interference. Scientists have conducted few studies of this kind, but it is possible that such interactions between species are common aspects of the chorus.

*The birds sing at dawn. What sounds to be*
*awakened by! If only our sleep, our dreams,*
*are such as to harmonize with the song, the*
*warbling, of the birds, ushering in the day.*
*— Henry David Thoreau*

*Yellow-breasted Chat*

*House Wren*

*Red-winged Blackbird (female)*

*A thousand birds . . . gently twittering and ushering in the light.*
— HENRY DAVID THOREAU

*Henslow's Sparrow*

Whether the chorus is organized or not, listening to it is a powerful experience. Who has not been affected, as Thoreau was (March 10, 1852), by those "ambrosial mornings . . . when a thousand birds were heard gently twittering and ushering in the light." Some listeners enjoy rising before dawn to hear the first singers of the day. Each species seems to chime in at a slightly different light level. Often the robins are the first to make themselves known, with other species sounding off in a somewhat regular sequence as dawn unfolds. It's fun to make a list — the first dozen singers are easy to discern, but as the chorus grows it becomes a challenge to detect newcomers. Even without knowing the songsters, the chorus is impressive. But when one learns to identify the participants, a greater pleasure emerges, as Arthur Allen discovered: "I listen to the chorus of voices on a May morning and pick out one friend after another as he announces his presence, his 'good morning,' if you will, to all his brothers and me. For now my ears bring to me even as much pleasure as my eyes, and I am sorry for those who do not hear."

Whatever the explanations, the dawn chorus is a remarkable medley of avian songs. It is especially prominent in northern temperate areas around the world, where a high proportion of songbirds have melodious songs. Inspired by this sunrise anthem of the birds, Longfellow imagined the chorus riding the crest of dawn like a wave, traveling uninterrupted across continents, round and round the planet, forevermore:

> *Think, every morning when the sun peeps through*
> *The dim leaf-latticed windows of the grove,*
> *How jubilant the happy birds renew*
> *Their old, melodious madrigals of love!*
> *And when you think of this, remember too*
> *'Tis always morning somewhere, and above*
> *The awakening continents, from shore to shore,*
> *Somewhere the birds are singing evermore.*
> — HENRY WADSWORTH LONGFELLOW

*Prothonotary Warbler (above and right)*

# Messages of the Poets

*When we embrace the words of our best nature poets, we discover a new world of perception, one that integrates observation with passionate and heartfelt interpretation. The best poets do not ignore scientific facts — they use them to their advantage, as stepping stones toward higher knowledge and love. The poets lead us into uncharted territory and help us expand our understanding and appreciation of nature. But how do their views differ from those of ordinary people? Why do their writings stir our emotions? What are their primary messages? And is there any pattern to their beliefs, any universal themes that they convey?*

The ultimate success of nature poetry is rooted in the poet's perception and appreciation of the moment, which provides a foundation for interpretation, if interpretation is necessary. Some writers attempt only to distill the moment with crystalline clarity, a worthy goal in itself. The haiku poets of Japan were masters of this, conveying experience with uncluttered simplicity. Yosa Buson's sparse words, for example, bring to life a clear, undistorted image: "Sparrow singing — its tiny mouth open." American poets were prone to greater wordiness, but nonetheless could evoke simple and powerful images. For instance, James Russell Lowell remains firmly rooted in an event, even though he adds a measure of emotional response:

> *As a twig trembles, which a bird*
> *Lights on to sing, then leaves unbent,*
> *So is my memory thrilled and stirred: —*
> *I only know she came and went.*

If one fails to perceive the details of the present moment, and is instead controlled by internal chatter that clouds the perception of natural events, then one hears not the messages inherent in nature, but only the echos of one's thoughts. This results in inferior nature poetry, where details of the moment are obscured by mental noise. I personally trust those writers whose lucid descriptions prove that they are looking and listening with a quiet mind — searching, exploring, and revealing nature's true patterns. If they do this well, then their deeper, more personal extractions of meaning can be trusted.

*A melancholy bird? Oh, idle thought!*
*In nature there is nothing melancholy.*
— SAMUEL TAYLOR COLERIDGE

*Gray Catbird*

Poets appreciate natural events within the context of their surroundings. In nature, nothing ever happens by itself. Every event, every bird song, occurs as part of a greater whole, and poets often strive to communicate this aspect in their verse. For example, consider Robert Frost's revealing observation that Ovenbird songs echo off nearby tree trunks ("The Ovenbird" 1916):

> *There is a singer everyone has heard,*
> *Loud, a mid-summer and mid-wood bird,*
> *Who makes the solid tree trunks sound again . . .*

The analytical mind tends to focus on isolated events, ignoring many aspects of the context. The poet usually works in the opposite direction — he or she is struck by a natural event and describes it by embracing the complete situation in which it occurs, allowing it to remain embedded in the environment. For instance, this explains why, when writing about the song of the Hermit Thrush, most poets refer to the quality of the forest in which they hear the song — the "deep secluded recesses" of Whitman, or Tolman's "deep, solemn wood." Scientists often study specific aspects of context in an attempt to elucidate cause and effect. Poets appreciate context because it is a crucial component of the human experience, and they often embrace flexible views of cause and effect.

Scientific analyses usually describe natural events mechanistically, with logical but narrowly defined explanations of cause and effect. For instance, most of us view bird song as being created by a physical entity we call a bird. The sound, we surmise, comes from an organ in the throat of the bird and is thrust from the bird into the environment. There is no possibility in our conceptual world for an opposite view — that bird song may be brought into being by aspects of the environment, sometimes unattached to a physical bird. Poets, on the other hand, often embrace such views and interpret natural events in mind-boggling ways. For instance, consider John Tabb's Eastern Bluebird creation tale, in which he describes the transfiguration of a flower first into sound and then into the form of the bird:

> *When God had made a host of them,*
> *One little flower still lacked a stem*
> *To hold its blossom blue;*
> *So into it, he breathed a song,*
> *And suddenly, with petals strong*
> *As wings, away it flew.*

Tabb purposely stretches reality so that he can portray a real aspect of our human experience — that bluebirds are, in a sense, flowers given voice and wings.

*Ovenbird*

*Louisiana Waterthrush*

*Eastern Bluebird*

Indeed, naturalists have long been impressed by the Eastern Bluebird's *turalee* call, which they considered an auditory harbinger of spring. Employing a different flower reference, Burroughs (1877) described it as "that first note of his in early spring—a note that may be called the violet of sound, heard above the cold, damp earth, as is its floral type to the eye a few weeks later." Thoreau was also moved, and his descriptions of the call include unusual views of cause and effect. On March 2, 1859, he wrote: "His soft warble melts in the ear, as the snow is melting in the valleys around. The bluebird comes and with his warble drills the ice and sets free the rivers and ponds and frozen ground." This image may be of little use to a scientist, but it sounds a powerful chord among those who are intimate with the bluebird's sweet note, when heard at winter's end. Through imaginative manipulation of cause and effect, Thoreau weds the bluebird's call to its surroundings.

Thoreau's most involved message concerning the *turalee* came on February 18, 1857, when he wrote that it exists in its own right, drawn into being by a complex juxtaposition of environmental factors on the leading edge of spring. Note, however, that on this particular day, the elements were not quite strong enough to materialize the call: "I am excited by the wonderful air and go listening for the note of the bluebird . . . The very grain of the air seems to have undergone a change and is ready to split into the form of the bluebird's warble. Methinks if it were visible, or I could cast some fine dust which would betray it, it would take a corresponding shape. The bluebird does not come till the air consents and his wedge will enter easily. The air over these fields is a foundry full of moulds for casting bluebird's warbles. Any sound uttered now would take that form, not of the harsh, vibrating, rending scream of the jay, but a softer, flowing, curling warble, like a purling stream of the lobes of flowing sand and clay. Here is the soft air, and the moist expectant apple trees, but not yet the bluebird. They do not quite attain to song."

Thoreau's interpretation might strike some as outlandish and impossible. But Thoreau and other poets court what seems impossible on purpose, in order to describe elements of the human experience that less imaginative writing fails to convey. Furthermore, it is possible that their unconventional views of cause and effect have merit—they may reflect aspects of reality that most of us simply do not perceive, or else refuse to consider because of inflexible beliefs. If we were able to truly understand nature, we might discover that it is the poets who come closest to revealing its actual form. Admittedly, science provides us with an amazing wealth of useful information, but thinking only from a scientific perspective might mask a greater reality, one that embraces art and religion as well as science—a reality that the enlightened poet struggles to reveal.

*American Redstart*

*Blue-winged Warbler*

Nature poets inhabit a world in which there is no clear separation of the seer from the seen or the listener from the sound. Most poets assume that humankind is a part of nature, inextricably connected to all natural events. Thoreau (February 20, 1857) makes this point with a "listening stone" analogy: "What is the relation between a bird and the ear that appreciates its melody, to whom, perchance, it is more charming and significant than any else? Certainly they are intimately related, and the one was made for the other. It is a natural fact. If I were to discover that a certain kind of stone by the pond-shore was affected, say partially disintegrated, by a particular natural sound, as of a bird or insect, I see that one could not be completely described without describing the other. I am that rock by the pondside." Thoreau a rock? . . . indeed! Yet being a listening stone did not prevent him from describing nature; it simply meant that he was also describing himself, for he was firmly interconnected to all that he observed. Thoreau celebrated this truth in his writing — that we humans are born into this world with a natural appreciation of bird songs, just as the birds themselves are born to sing.

In scientific studies, nature's objects and events are described dispassionately, without emotion, presumably devoid of personal feeling or bias — like a stone un-affected. The poet's attitude toward nature is usually sympathetic. For poets, it is natural and necessary to feel and be affected, and it is okay to let emotional response color one's observations. The poet is a stone admitting its own disintegration, and then letting the disintegration stoke the fire of creativity. The poet embraces the natural world with passion, as one might embrace a lover, knowing that the purest love involves a direct appreciation of that which is loved. This is perhaps

*My bedroom, when I awoke this morning, was full of bird-songs, which is the greatest pleasure in life.*
— ROBERT LOUIS STEVENSON

*Carolina Chickadee*

Why are we soothed by the songs of birds? Do we learn this reponse, or is it more deeply ingrained, perhaps even a part of our genetic heritage? For countless centuries, humankind has awakened to the twittering of birds, the gentle and pleasant medley of nature that begs us from sleep and reminds us we are alive and well. Could it be that we have developed, deep within our beings, an expectation, and perhaps a need, to hear these melodies? Do bird songs help us affirm our place in nature? Does hearing them impart a sense of security that helps us face the challenges of the day? If the answers are "yes," then haiku poet Issa sensed the truth when he surmised that "birds sing the music of heaven in this world," and it is no wonder that Chaucer was so moved by their songs:

> *Herkneth this blisful briddes how they singe,*
> *And see the fresshe floures how they springe:*
> *Full is myn herte of revel and solas.*

We protect what we love. Given the great concern in modern times over the preservation of nature, it is important that we foster a sense of connectedness to the natural world. Science is marvelously effective at providing us with details that enhance our appreciation of nature, whereas poetry deals more directly with issues of sympathy, feeling, and love. When poetry and prose are resonant with scientific fact, they become wonderfully effective tools for connecting, or rather re-connecting, humans to nature. They foster a superior kind of love, the kind of love Leonardo da Vinci described when he said, "For in truth great love is born of great knowledge of the thing loved." The greatest knowledge integrates human passion and emotion with scientific fact. Perhaps better than anyone, the poets illuminate nature, elucidate our experience of it, and foster a deep appreciation and love for all of its manifestations, including the songs of birds.

For those who genuinely appreciate bird song, who feel it in their bones and hear it in their hearts, the prospect of Rachel Carson's "silent spring" is frightening indeed. Those who love the songs of birds, who are emotionally affected by them, will do everything in their power to keep nature's voice alive and well. The poets tell us that bird song is an elixir to our soul, and if we listen with our hearts we know that this is true. For, as Ms. Parker so clearly stated over a century ago:

> *Would not half the joy of a spring morning be lost if*
> *their glad notes were silent? Would not the burdens of*
> *noonday seem heavier if no bird voice cheered us? And*
> *the evening shadows fall darker and sadder if they sang*
> *us no good-night melodies?*
> — CAROLINE H. PARKER

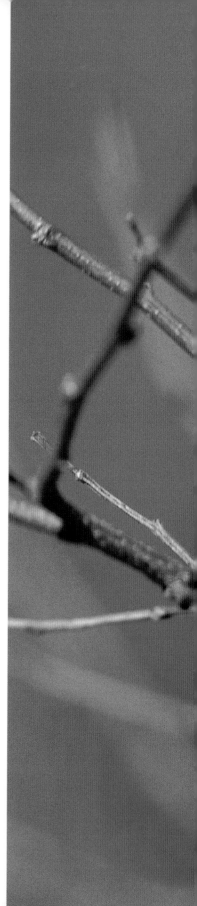

*Song Sparrow*

# Spirit of Listening

*Spring arrives — the forests, fields, and marshes come alive with the sounds of birds. Every walk in nature reveals new species, each with its own song. But the variety is overwhelming. Learning each bird's notes seems such an impossible task. Is it really worth the trouble? Can't one enjoy the medley without knowing all the singers? Will analyzing nature's choir take away from its magic, or will it add a new dimension to one's appreciation? And if it does increase enjoyment, then how does one go about learning the songs, and what frame of mind will make the task easier and more satisfying?*

The joy of recognizing each bird's voice has been celebrated by countless naturalists. Wilson Flagg (1881) extolls the benefits: "The music of birds, though delightful to all, conveys active and durable pleasure only to those who have learned to associate with their notes, in connection with the scenes of nature, a crowd of interesting and romantic images. To many persons of this character it affords more delight than the most brilliant music of the concert or opera." Arthur Allen (1930), too, conveys the potential for delight: "And now I think over how, one by one, I learned the different calls of the wild folk until the hubbub changed to music, and the morning chorus, instead of being a disturbance, became a joy to be looked forward to and long remembered."

Great pleasure results when we learn to identify the songs of common birds in our surroundings. But many people, especially those of an artistic temperament, often resist learning. "Why should I bother to learn the songs," they ask, "when I can appreciate the chorus without knowing any of the birds?" Without doubt, unskilled listeners can and do appreciate the chorus, but it seems an appreciation of a lesser kind. To the naive ear, the sounds all mix together to create a pleasurable sensation, but this is like listening to an orchestra without knowing the different musical instruments. Variations, such as the presence or absence of certain species in the chorus, go largely unnoticed. And specific sounds do not stand out to the listener or evoke pleasant memories, if they are perceived at all. People who lack a basic knowledge of bird song often do not hear subtle bird sounds that literally jump out at the experienced listener — their ears may hear these sounds, but their minds do not perceive them as different.

*Lacking the heart-room, the song lies dead;*
*Half is the song that reaches the ear,*
*Half is the hearing.*
                — SAMUEL A. HARPER

In all arts and crafts, it is important to know the palette of creative possibilities. The painter must be familiar with colors, the musician must know the notes, and the poet must understand words — otherwise they cannot create good works or fully grasp the creations of others. Likewise, the nature enthusiast must know nature's many voices. The ability to discriminate makes us susceptible to the full range of impressions that the natural world offers, providing the basis for our appreciation. As we learn to identify the songs of birds, our experience of the avian soundscape expands and becomes more powerful, as William Hamilton Gibson noted in his book *Strolls by Starlight and Sunshine* (1891): "What an endless diversion, this picturesque, kaleidoscope music, this pastoral opera, every fresh recognition bringing its vision of some favorite feathered songster, each with its welcome personal reminiscence."

To learn bird song, it is important to spend as much time as possible outdoors. As Wordsworth put it: "Come forth into the light of things. Let Nature be your Teacher." The learning aids mentioned later in this chapter are meant to be adjunct tools only — they are no substitute for actual experience in nature. By doing most of our learning outdoors, we see and hear birds in their surroundings and form memories and impressions of each. Whenever possible, find the singer and watch it make its music. Such experiences are rarely forgotten. If you can, visit natural areas, away from the distractions of civilization. As Bradford Torrey wrote in 1885: "You hear a song in the village street and pass along umoved; but stand in the silence of the forest, with your feet in a bed of creeping snowberry and oxalis, and the same song goes to your soul." Emerson, too, valued nature's sanctuary:

> *If I could put my woods in song*
> *And tell what's there enjoyed,*
> *All men would to my garden throng,*
> *And leave the cities void.*

Books and other learning tools are useful, but not as the dominant methods of learning. As Burroughs advised: "Ornithology cannot be learned satisfactorily from books. The satisfaction is learning it from nature. One must have an original experience with the birds. The books are only a guide, the invitation." Likewise, Wordsworth begs us to shelve our books and head into nature with an open heart:

> *Enough of Science and of Art;*
> *Close up these barren leaves;*
> *Come forth, and bring with you a heart*
> *That watches and receives.*

*Dark-eyed Junco*

*Common Yellowthroat*

*An incantation so serene,*
*So innocent, befits the scene:*
*There's magic in that small bird's note —*
*See, there he flits — the yellow-throat.*
— HENRY VAN DYKE

It is truly important to listen from the heart, to allow ourselves to be moved by what we hear. In the words of Solomon Ibn-Gabirol (eleventh-century Spain): "Of what avail is an open eye, if the heart is blind?" Doesn't the same hold true for the ear? Samuel Harper (1917) asssserted " 'Tis Eden everywhere to hearts that listen," and wrote these revealing lines:

*Lacking the heart-room the song lies dead;*
*Half is the song that reaches the ear,*
*Half is the hearing.*

Approaching nature in a receptive frame of mind, we cannot help but expand our knowledge and heighten our appreciation. However, it is vital that we be patient in our quest to observe birds. While some birds are easy to find and watch, there are many more that foil our attempts to see them, singing from dense foliage high in trees or in shrubby thickets. Christopher Cranch (1904) makes this point:

*Dear hidden bird, full oft I've heard*
*Your pleasant invitation;*
*And searched for you amid your boughs*
*With fruitless observation.*

*Prairie Warbler*

*White-eyed Vireo*

*Gray Catbird*

Elusive species are difficult to spot, and it may be a waste of time to pursue them in hopes of a good view. In fact, sometimes it's best to just sit and wait, relaxing on a stump or boulder in the woods. For, as Emerson observed:

> *Oft didst thou thread the woods in vain*
> *To find what bird had piped the strain.*
> *Seek not, and the little eremite*
> *Flies gayly forth and sings in sight.*

Sometimes, it takes years to discover the source of a song, especially one rarely heard. But this should be welcome because it adds an element of mystery to the learning process. Mysteries grow more powerful as one's knowledge expands. In other words, great enjoyment results when mysteries occur against the background of the known — the more one knows, the more potent and alluring each unknown becomes. And, even when you finally identify an elusive singer, it will occupy a special place in your mind. As Aldo Leopold said in *A Sand County Almanac:* "There is a peculiar virtue in the music of elusive birds. Songsters that sing from topmost boughs are easily seen and easily forgotten; they have the mediocrity of the obvious. What one remembers is the invisible hermit thrush pouring silver chords from impenetrable shadows." Wordsworth similarly praised his native cuckoo, which he often heard but seldom saw:

> *Thrice welcome, darling of the spring.*
> *Even yet thou art to me*
> *No bird, but an invisible thing,*
> *A voice, a mystery.*

Bradford Torrey noted: "Every bird's voice has something characteristic about it, just as every human voice has tones and inflections which those who are familiar with its owner, will infallibly detect." We would be endlessly confused if every individual bird had a totally unique voice. Fortunately, this is not the case. Even though individuals within a species often sing unique interpretations, their songs almost always conform to a broader "species pattern" that humans can easily learn.

The situation is complicated, however, by the existence of regional differences in song patterns within species. Such "song dialects," as they are called, are commonplace. For example, Northern Cardinals and Red-winged Blackbirds in a particular region usually share a number of song patterns and sound much alike; those living hundreds of miles away share different song patterns and sound noticeably different. Despite these regional variations, all the songs of a species still

*Northern Cardinal*

possess qualities that allow human listeners and the birds themselves to recognize them. It is usually easy to identify the songs of familiar species, even when you encounter them in areas where they sound a little different.

Another complication is that young birds often sing incomplete or sloppy versions of songs, especially in autumn or early spring when they are first learning to sing. Such "subsongs" are difficult to identify without catching sight of the singer. One writer referred to these as "songs yet half devised in the dim drear first beginnings of the year." Luckily for humans, young birds learn quickly and soon conform to the adult pattern. (Note: Song learning is a complex topic not addressed in this book. Refer to the texts listed on page 133 for more information).

Although outdoor learning is best, various teaching aids can hasten one's development. Perhaps the most useful are audio guides to bird songs and calls. These allow you to hear bird sounds indoors and review them during the winter months, in anticipation of spring's chorus. They also let you hear species you've never heard, perhaps as you prepare for trips to new areas. And they inform you about special songs that are rarely heard, thus encouraging you to listen for them during your excursions in the field.

Audio guides are fine learning resources, but they are not intended as substitutes for hearing and seeing birds in natural settings. From a poetic standpoint, it is imperative to experience song in the context of its surroundings. This important element is missing from recorded songs! In a sense, recorded songs are like "caged songs," giving added meaning to Hawkes' poem about caged birds:

> *My aviary is the good green wood,*
> *I would not cage its songsters if I could.*
> *Sweeter the song of one wild bird to me*
> *Than all the notes in sad captivity.*

Other useful tools include books and multimedia guides to birds and their sounds. Interactive CD-ROMs, DVDs, and similar formats are already making the learning process easier by allowing one to hear a bird's sounds, see corresponding photographs and videos, and quiz oneself in unique and effective ways. At some point, there might even be portable devices that will identify the songs of common birds for you. One cannot help but wonder if this will be an asset or a liability to developing a skilled ear.

Learning aides may also be of the homespun variety. For instance, naturalists often keep field notebooks in which they they include notes, sketches, poems, and the like. Keeping a record of each species' song is worthwhile, especially when you first identify it in the field — a concise description of the song and the habitat will

*Nashville Warbler*

*Chestnut-sided Warbler*

help you remember. A list of verbal, nonsense-word, or onomatopoiec mnemonic devices will also help you remember songs; these can be taken from field guides and books or devised from one's own encounters with birds. Sometimes, it's even helpful to make "sound pictures" that reveal critical aspects of one's personal experience of a song—for example, an inward spiral might be drawn to represent the Veery's song, or simple lines sketched to depict the pitch changes and cadence of the White-throated Sparrow's song. If suitably inspired, one can even write poems and prose in an attempt to capture the emotional depth and feelings inspired by encounters with singing birds.

Learning to identify and appreciate the songs of birds is a lifelong pursuit. Though important, identification by itself is just one of several prerequisites for enjoyment. Even more important is attitude, one's state of mind. Every bird we encounter offers something new to us and every song we hear is a special event, occuring in a natural context that is a unique expression of the moment. The person capable of the greatest enjoyment is the one who can seize each experience and enjoy it to the fullest. To reach this goal, we must empty ourselves of mental chatter and open ourselves fully, with heartfelt sympathy, to all the songs of nature. This is no easy task. For, as Thoreau reminds us (October 26, 1853):

> *How watchful we must be to keep the*
> *crystal well that we are made, clear!*
> — HENRY DAVID THOREAU

*Northern Parula*

*Black-and-white Warbler*

# The Compact Disc

The compact disc that accompanies this book will allow you to hear most of the bird songs discussed — they are arranged in the same order as in the text. Each recording is track-coded for rapid access, and each track is introduced by a short narrative that describes what you will hear. Refer to the list below for species and tracks.

A special compact disc entitled *Songbird Portraits* is available for those interested in hearing high-quality stereo recordings *without narration* that feature our most beautiful bird songs. This disc is described on the last page of this book, along with ordering instructions. Other nonnarrated compact discs by Lang Elliott can be found at *www.naturesound.com*.

*Note:* The numbers below are equivalent to the track numbers on the compact disc. All recordings depict typical song unless otherwise specified.

## Nature's Finest Songsters

1. Hermit Thrush
2. Wood Thrush
3. Swainson's Thrush
4. Veery
5. Thrush songs slowed down
6. Carolina Wren
7. Winter Wren
8. Bewick's Wren
9. Canyon Wren
10. Bachman's Sparrow
11. Song Sparrow
12. Lark Sparrow
13. Fox Sparrow
14. White-throated Sparrow
15. House Finch
16. Purple Finch
17. Northern Mockingbird
18. Brown Thrasher
19. Gray Catbird
20. Eastern Meadowlark
21. Western Meadowlark
22. Bobolink
23. American Robin
24. Rose-breasted Grosbeak
25. Scarlet Tanager
26. Summer Tanager
27. Northern Cardinal
28. Baltimore Oriole

## Lesser Musicians

29. Henslow's Sparrow
30. Grasshopper Sparrow
31. Savannah Sparrow
32. Field Sparrow
33. Eastern Phoebe
34. Empidonax Flycatchers
    (Least, Acadian, Willow, & Alder)
35. Eastern Wood-Pewee
36. Tufted Titmouse
37. Black-capped Chickadee (song & calls)
38. White-breasted Nuthatch
39. House Wren
40. Blue Jay (calls)
41. American Crow (calls)
42. Common Grackle
43. Red-winged Blackbird
44. Red-eyed Vireo

**Flight Songs and Night Songs** (and other special songs)

45. Ovenbird (typical & flight song)
46. Common Yellowthroat (typical & flight song)
47. Vesper Sparrow (typical & flight song)
48. Western Meadowlark (typical & flight song)
49. Bobolink (extended flight song)
50. Skylark (flight song)
51. Horned Lark (typical & flight song)
52. Sprague's Pipit (flight song)
53. Gray Catbird (night singing)
54. Sedge Wren (night singing)
55. Marsh Wren (night singing)
56. Eastern Wood-Pewee (dawn song)
57. Acadian Flycatcher (typical & dawn song)
58. Western Kingbird (dawn song)
59. Northern Parula (typical & dawn song)
60. Blue-winged Warbler (typical & dawn song)
61. Black-throated Green Warbler (typical & dawn song)
62. Field Sparrow (typical & dawn song)
63. Chipping Sparrow (typical & dawn song)
64. American Robin (dawn song)
65. House Finch (excited courtship song)
66. Purple Finch (anti-predator song)
67. Grasshopper Sparrow (typical & complex song)
68. Tufted Titmouse (countersinging & song matching)
69. Wood Thrush (countersinging & song mismatching)
70. Red-winged Blackbird (male/female duet)
71. Brown-headed Cowbird (male/female duet)
72. Northern Mockingbird (song with mimicry)
73. European Starling (song with mimicry)
74. Yellow-breasted Chat (song with mimicry)

**Additional Tracks**

75. Eastern Bluebird (song & *turalee* call)
76. Closing Comments (see Page 136 for
    description of *Songbird Portraits* CD)

*Hermit Thrush*

# Photo and Sound Credits

Most of the 135 photographs featured in this book are by Lang Elliott. They were taken using a Canon EOS system, including a 500 mm *f*/4.5 lens coupled with a 1.4x teleconverter. A Gitzo tripod was used along with an Arca Swiss Monoball head. All images are ambient light exposures. Some subjects were attracted and enticed to sing by playing recordings of songs. Most shots were obtained with the help of a DB Design portable photographer's blind.

In addition to the author's work, thirteen images from other photographers were used (T = top, B = bottom):

Mark Bilak — 93T
Mazlowki Photos — 69
Marie Read — 38, 44B, 57, 70
Carl Sams II — 36B, 39
Brian Small — 37B, 53T, 71, 72T, 119T
Tom Vezo — 73T

Most field recordings on the compact disc were made by Lang Elliott using a portable Sony TCD-D10 Pro DAT recorder and various microphones, including a Sennheiser MKH-20 mounted in a Dan Gibson sound parabola and a Sennheiser MKH-70 shotgun microphone. Additional recordings were provided by Ted Mack, Bill Evans, Kevin Colver, Jeff Wells, and Jean Roché. The accompanying compact disc was produced by the author using Digidesign Pro-Tools audio editing hardware and software.

*Yellow-headed Blackbird*

*Dickcissel*

# Sources: Author List

Below are listed the naturalists, poets, writers, and ornithologists who are quoted in this book, arranged alphabetically, with short descriptions and lifespans.

Allen, Arthur A. — American ornithologist and writer 1885–1964

Bailey, Liberty Hyde — American botanist and philosopher 1858–1954

Ball, Alice Eliza — American naturalist and writer 1867–?

Bent, Arthur Cleveland — American ornithologist 1866–1954

Browning, Elizabeth Barrett — English poet 1806–1861

Browning, Robert — English poet 1812–1889

Bryant, William Cullen — American poet 1794–1878

Burroughs, John — American naturalist and writer 1837–1921

Buson, Yosa — Japanese haiku poet 1716–1784

Byron, Lord George Gordon — English poet 1788–1824

Catesby, Mark — American Colonial naturalist and writer 1683–1749

Chapman, Frank — American ornithologist 1864–1945

Chaucer, Geoffrey — English poet 1340?–1400

Coleridge, Samuel Taylor — English poet and critic 1772–1834

Cooke, Wells Woodbridge — American ornithologist 1858–1916

Cranch, Christopher Pearse — Amer. transcendentalist and poet 1813–1892

da Vinci, Leonardo — Italian artist, architect, and philospher 1425–1519

Dickinson, Emily — American poet 1830–1886

Dorr, Eben Pearson — no information found

Emerson, Ralph Waldo — American philospher and poet 1803–1882

Flagg, Wilson — American naturalist and writer 1805–1884

Forbush, Edward — American ornithologist 1858–1929

Fowler, W. Warde — American historian and naturalist 1847–1921

Frost, Robert — American poet 1875–1963

Gibson, William Hamilton — Amer. artist and nature writer 1850–1896

Gray, Thomas — English poet 1716–1771

Hardy, Thomas — English poet and novelist 1840–1928

Harper, Samuel Alain — American naturalist and writer 1875–?

Hawkes, Clarence — American naturalist and writer 1869–?

Hoffmann, Ralph — American botanist and ornithologist 1870–1932

Holmes, Oliver Wendell — American wit, poet, and novelist 1809–1894

Howe, Reginald Heber — American scientist and ornithologist 1875–?

Ibn-Gabirol, Solomon — Eleventh-century Spanish poet

Issa, Kobayashi — Japanese haiku poet 1763–1827

Keyser, Leander Sylvester — American naturalist and writer 1856–?

Krutch, Joseph Wood — American naturalist and writer 1893–1970

Larcom, Lucy — American poet 1824–1893

Lawrence, Louise de Kiriline — American ornithologist 1894–?

Leggett, Benjamin Franklin — American poet 1834–?

Leopold, Aldo — American conservationist 1886–1948

Longfellow, Henry Wadsworth — American poet and scholar 1807–1882

Lowell, James Russell — American poet and critic 1819–1891

Mathews, Ferdinand Schuyler — Amer. naturalist and writer 1854–1938

Miller, Olive Thorne — American naturalist and writer 1831–1918

Mills, John Proctor — American poet 1879–1965

Muir, John — American naturalist, explorer, and writer 1838–1914

Parker, Caroline H. — American naturalist and writer (lifespan not known)

Parkhurst, Howard Elmore — American naturalist and writer 1848–1916

Peterson, Roger Tory — American ornithologist and artist 1908–1996

Rumi, Jelaluddin — Persian poet and mystic 1207–1273

Scollard, Clinton — American poet 1860–1932

Seton, Ernest Thompson — American naturalist and writer 1860–1946

Shakespeare, William — English poet and dramatist 1564–1616

Shelley, Percy Bysshe — English poet 1792–1822

Stanton, Frank Lebby — American editor and verse writer 1857–1927

Stedman, Edmund Clarence — American poet 1833–1908

Stevenson, Robert Louis — Scottish novelist, essayist, and poet 1850–1894

Tabb, John Bannister — American gnomic poet 1845–1909

Thomas, Edith Matilda — American verse writer 1854–1925

Thoreau, Henry David — Amer. naturalist, poet, and essayist 1817–1862

Tolman, Emily — American poet (lifespan not known)

Torrey, Bradford — American naturalist and writer 1845–1912

Trowbridge, John Townsend — American novelist and poet 1827–1916

Van Dyke, Henry — American minister, poet, and essayist 1852–1933

West, A. — American naturalist and poet (lifespan not known)

White, Gilbert — English naturalist and writer 1720–1793

Whitman, Walt — American poet 1819–1892

Wilde, Richard Henry — American lawyer and verse writer 1789–1847

Wilson, Alexander — American ornithologist and poet 1766–1813

Wordsworth, William — English poet 1770–1850

# Sources: Quotations by Chapter

**Note:** Quotations are listed below, arranged by chapter and page number in text.

**Quotations by Henry David Thoreau:** I do not include complete Thoreau references in the listing below. All quotes by Thoreau were taken from his Journals and are referenced in the book text and below by Journal entry date. All of these can be found in the following standard reference: *Journal: The Writings of Henry D. Thoreau.* Volumes 1–5. John C. Broderick, general editor. Princeton, New Jersey: Princeton University Press, 1981–1997. In addition, Thoreau's Journal entries that refer specifically to birds are arranged by species in the following useful reference: *Thoreau on Birds: Notes on New England Birds from the Journals of Henry David Thoreau.* Edited by Francis H. Allen. Boston: Beacon Press, 1993.

**Quotations by John Burroughs:** Date references in the text refer to the first copyrights on each book title, especially *Wake Robin,* 1871. Below, all quotes are referenced by page to later, more standard editions, especially the Riverside Press series published by Houghton Mifflin and Company.

## PREFACE

8. **"The good New…"** Liberty Hyde Bailey. *The Nature-Study Idea.* New York: Doubleday, Page and Company, 1903. Page 21.

9. **"O there's a song…"** Clarence Hawkes. *Tenants of the Trees.* Boston: L. C. Page and Company, 1907. Page 130.

## WHY BIRDS SING

11. **"The birds pour…"** William Wordsworth. "Devotional Incitements," lines 17–18 (poem written in 1832). *The Complete Poetical Works of William Wordsworth.* Boston: Houghton Mifflin Company, 1904. Page 696.

12. **"For, what are the…"** Robert Browning. "Pippa Passes: Part IV, Night" (poem first published in 1835). *Browning: Poetical Works 1833–1864.* London: Oxford University Press, 1970. Page 358.

15. **"The birds I heard…"** Henry David Thoreau (March 4, 1840)

15. **"The language of…"** Gilbert White. "Letter XLIII dated Sept. 9, 1778." *The Gilbert White Museum Edition of The Natural History of Selborne by Gilbert White.* London: Shepheard-Walwyn, 1977 (the Natural History was first published in 1789). Page 116.

17. **"As long as…"** John Muir. Quoted in *In Nature's Heart: The Wilderness Days of John Muir.* Edited by Linda Landan with photographs by James Randklev. The Nature Company, 1991. Page 79.

20. **"There can be…"** Liberty Hyde Bailey. *The Nature-Study Idea.* New York: Doubleday, Page and Company, 1903. Page 121.

20. **"sing the music…"** Kobayashi Issa. *The Essential Haiku: Versions of Basho, Buson, and Issa.* Edited by Robert Hass. Hopewell, New Jersey: The Ecco Press, 1994. Page 221.

20. **"Hard is the hert…"** Geoffrey Chaucer. "The Romaunt of the Rose," lines 85–89 (written circa 1365). *The Poetical Works of Geoffrey Chaucer,* vol. 6. London: Bell and Daldy, 1866. Page 3.

## NATURE'S FINEST SONGSTERS

23. **"And where the…"** Henry Wadsworth Longfellow. Quoted in *Our Friends, the Birds* by Caroline H. Parker. Chicago: A. Flanagan, 1897. Page 137.

24. **"Great Nature had…"** Henry Van Dyke. "The Pipes O' Pan." *The Poems of Henry Van Dyke.* New York: Charles Scribner's Sons, 1911. Page 249.

24. **"If we take…"** John Burroughs. *The Writings of John Burroughs I: Wake Robin.* Boston: Houghton, Mifflin and Company. The Riverside Press, Cambridge. Copyrights 1871, 1876, 1895, 1904, and 1913. Page 25.

24. **"serene religious…"** John Burroughs (see above). Page 51.

24. **"O spheral…"** John Burroughs (see above). Page 52.

26. **"O liquid free…"** Walt Whitman. "When Lilacs Last in the Dooryard Bloom'd," lines 104–105 (poem first published in 1865). *Leaves of Grass.* Boston: James R. Osgood and Company, 1881. Page 255.

26. **"thus to fling…"** Thomas Hardy. "The Darkling Thrush" (written in 1900). *Thomas Hardy: Poems of the Past and the Present.* London: Macmillan and Company, Ltd., New York: The Macmillan Company, 1903 (first edition 1901). Page 169.

26. **"From deep secluded…"** Walt Whitman. "When Lilacs Last in the Dooryard Bloom'd," lines 119–120 (poem first published in 1865). *Leaves of Grass.* Boston: James R. Osgood and Company, 1881. Page 255.

27. **"This bird never…"** Henry David Thoreau (July 5, 1852).

27. **"And where the…"** Henry Wadsworth Longfellow. Quoted in *Our Friends, the Birds* by Caroline H. Parker. Chicago: A. Flanagan, 1897. Page 137.

27. **"Like liquid pearls…"** John Townsend Trowbridge. "The Pewee," lines 74–76. *The Poetical Works of John Townsend Trowbridge.* Boston: Houghton, Mifflin and Company, 1903. Page 14.

27. **"When we are…"** Wilson Flagg. *A Year With the Birds; or, The Birds and Seasons of New England.* Boston: Educational Publishing Company. 1881, Page 129.

29. **"The Veery's mysterious…"** Frank Chapman. *Bird Life.* New York: D. Appleton and Company, 1897. Page 254.

29. **"And when my…"** Henry Van Dyke. "The Veery," lines 29–32. *The Builders and other Poems by Henry Van Dyke.* New York: Charles Scribner's Sons, 1897. Page 29.

29. **"more under the…"** John Burroughs. *The Writings of John Burroughs IX: Riverby.* Boston: Houghton, Mifflin and Company. The Riverside Press, Cambridge. Copyrights 1894, 1895, and 1904. Page 51.

29. **"As I come…"** Henry David Thoreau (June 22, 1853).

29. **"In the deep…"** Emily Tolman. Quoted in *Birds of Song and Story* by Elizabeth and Joseph Grinnell. Chicago: A. W. Mumford. 1901. Page 44.

30. **"Lilac and star…"** Walt Whitman. "When Lilacs last in the Dooryard Bloom'd," lines 205–206 (poem first published in 1865). *Leaves of Grass.* Boston: James R. Osgood and Company, 1881. Page 255.

30. **"a tremulous…"** John Burroughs. *The Writings of John Burroughs I: Wake Robin.* Boston: Houghton, Mifflin and Company. The Riverside Press, Cambridge. Copyrights 1871, 1876, 1895, 1904, and 1913. Page 48.

30. **"the silence was…"** John Burroughs (see above). Page 21.

30. **"exceptionally brisk…"** Henry David Thoreau (July 10, 1858).

31. "a cascade of..." Ralph Hoffman. *Birds of the Pacific States.* Boston: Houghton Mifflin Company, 1927. Page 242.

32. "I thought the..." Ralph Waldo Emerson. "Each and All," lines 13–14. *Poems* by Ralph Waldo Emerson. Boston: Houghton, Mifflin and Company, 1904 (first copyright 1867). Page 4.

32. "the true harbinger..." Wilson Flagg. *A Year With the Birds; or, The Birds and Seasons of New England.* Boston: Educational Publishing Company, 1881. Page 12.

32. "That's a cheerful..." Arthur A. Allen and Peter Paul Kellogg. Narration on side 2 of *Songbirds of America.* Published by Houghton Mifflin Company in the United States and elsewhere and by the Federation of Ontario Naturalists in Canada, 1954, 1963.

32. "Of all the..." John Burroughs. *The Heart of Burroughs's Journals.* Edited by Clara Barrus. Boston: Houghton Mifflin Company, 1928. Page 83.

35. "remarkable for its..." F. Schuyler Mathews. *Familiar Features of the Roadside.* New York: D. Appleton and Company, 1897. Page 172.

35. "disappoints one..." John Burroughs. *The Writings of John Burroughs I: Wake Robin.* Boston and New York: Houghton, Mifflin and Company. The Riverside Press, Cambridge. Copyrights 1871, 1876, 1895, 1904, and 1913. Page 78.

35. "Hark! 'tis our..." A. West. "Northern Nightingale." Quoted in *Twelve Months with the Birds and Poets* by Samuel A. Harper. Chicago: R. F. Seymour, 1917. Page 156.

35. "His song approaches..." John Burroughs. *The Writings of John Burroughs I: Wake Robin.* Boston: Houghton, Mifflin and Company. The Riverside Press, Cambridge. Copyrights 1871, 1876, 1895, 1904, and 1913. Page 62.

35. "sing more than..." Henry David Thoreau (May 24, 1855).

35. "Of all the..." Howard Elmore Parkhurst. *The Bird's Calendar.* New York: Charles Scribner's Sons, 1894. Page 234.

36. "The Indians..." Mark Catesby. *The Natural History of Carolina, Florida, and the Bahama Islands,* vol. 1. Printed at the expense of the author, 1731. Plate 27: The Mock-bird.

36. "There come a..." Frank L. Stanton. "The Mocking-bird." *Songs of the Soil.* New York: D. Appleton. 1894. Page 158.

37. "gifted with the..." Anonymous. "To the Catbird." quoted in *The Bird-Lover's Anthology,* compiled by Clinton Scollard and Jessie B. Brittenhouse. Boston: Houghton Mifflin Company, 1930. Page 140.

37. "After long days..." Clinton Scollard. "A Rain Song." Quoted in *Our Friends, the Birds* by Caroline H. Parker. Chicago: A. Flanagan, 1897. Page 123.

39. "Why, I'd give..." James Russell Lowell. "She Came and Went." *The Poetical Works of James Russell Lowell, in Four Volumes,* vol. 1. Boston: Houghton, Mifflin and Company. Copyrights 1848, 1876, and 1890. Page 245.

41. "The robin warbled..." William Cullen Bryant. Quoted in *Our Birds and their Nestlings* by Margaret Coulson Walker. New York: American Book Company, 1904. Page 26.

41. "a mad, reckless..." F. Schuyler Mathews. *Field Book of Wild Birds and their Music.* New York: G. P. Putnam's Sons, 1904. Page 49.

41. "Bob-o'-link..." William Cullen Bryant. "Robert of Lincoln." *Poetical Works of William Cullen Bryant.* New York: D. Appleton and Company, 1893. Page 229.

41. "a bubbling delirium..." Arthur Cleveland Bent. *Life Histories of North American Blackbirds, Orioles, Tanagers, and Allies.* United States National Museum Bulletin 211. Washington, D. C.: Smithsonian Institution, 1958. Page 44.

41. "It is as if..." Henry David Thoreau (June 1, 1857).

43. "The Robin is..." Wilson Flagg. *A Year With the Birds; or, The Birds and Seasons of New England.* Boston: Educational Publishing Company, 1881. Page 63.

43. "One of the..." Clarence Hawkes. *Tenants of the Trees.* Boston: L. C. Page and Company, 1907. Page 3.

43. "when birds and..." James Russell Lowell. "To A Dandelion." *The Poetical Works of James Russell Lowell, in Four Volumes,* vol. 1. Boston: Houghton, Mifflin and Company. Copyrights 1848, 1876, and 1890. Page 226.

43. "Did he sing..." Henry David Thoreau (April 21, 1852).

43. "How round and..." John Burroughs. *The Writings of John Burroughs I: Wake Robin.* Boston: Houghton, Mifflin and Company. The Riverside Press, Cambridge. Copyrights 1871, 1876, 1895, 1904, and 1913. Page 6.

43. "The sweetest sound..." Edmund Clarence Stedman. "Seeking the May-Flower" *The Poetical Works of Edmund Clarence Stedman.* Boston: Houghton, Mifflin and Company. Copyrights 1860, 1863, 1869, 1873, 1877, 1884, 1888, and 1891. Page 389.

44. "At first you..." Leander S. Keyser. *In Bird Land.* Chicago: A. C. McClurg and Company, 1897. Page 73.

44. "The cardinal's song..." Howard Elmore Parkhurst. *The Bird's Calendar.* New York: Charles Scribner's Sons, 1894. Page 218.

46. "cheering his labor..." James Russell Lowell. "The Nest." *The Poetical Works of James Russell Lowell, in Four Volumes,* vol. 4. Boston: Houghton, Mifflin and Company. Copyrights 1848, 1876, and 1890. Page 163.

46. "There's a song..." John Proctor Mills. Quoted in *Alabama Bird Day Book.* Department of Conservation. Montgomery, Alabama, 1923. Page 68.

46. "the original type..." John Burroughs. *The Writings of John Burroughs III: Birds and Poets.* Boston: Houghton Mifflin Company. Riverside Press, Cambridge. Copyrights 1877, 1895, and 1904. Page 4..

*Black-and-white Warbler*

*House Wren*

**46.** "serene exaltation…" John Burroughs. *The Writings of John Burroughs I: Wake Robin.* Boston: Houghton, Mifflin and Company. The Riverside Press, Cambridge. Copyrights 1871, 1876, 1895, 1904, and 1913. Page 75.

**46.** "Teach us, sprite…" Percy Bysshe Shelley. "To a Skylark," lines 61–65 (first published in 1820). *The Complete Poetical Works of Percy Bysshe Shelley, Centenary Edition in Four Volumes,* vol. 3. Boston: Houghton, Mifflin and Company, 1892. Page 270.

## LESSER MUSICIANS

**49.** "It is with birds…" Bradford Torrey. *Birds in the Bush.* Boston: Houghton, Mifflin and Company, 1885. Page 158.

**49.** "The ignorant and…" Wilson Flagg. *A Year With the Birds; or, The Birds and Seasons of New England.* Boston: Educational Publishing Company, 1881. Page 7.

**49.** "for those whose…" Samuel Harper. *Twelve Months with the Birds and Poets.* Chicago: R. F. Seymour, 1917. Page 20.

**49.** "Bird notes, with…" Samuel Harper (see above). Page 21.

**49.** "the poorest vocal…" Roger Tory Peterson. *A Field Guide to the Birds.* Boston: Houghton Mifflin Company, 1939. Page 144.

**50.** "In Conant's orchard…" Henry David Thoreau (June 14, 1851).

**50.** "A bubble of music…" Lucy Larcom. "The Field Sparrow." *The Poetical Works of Lucy Larcom.* Boston: Houghton, Mifflin and Company. Copyrights 1868, 1874, 1875, and 1880. Page 232.

**52.** "A pensive strain…" Edward Forbush. *Birds of Massachusetts and other New England States,* vol. 3. Norwood, Massachusetts: Berwick and Smith Company, 1929. Page 83.

**52.** "Phoebe! is all…" James Russell Lowell. "Phoebe." *The Poetical Works of James Russell Lowell, in Four Volumes,* vol. 4. Boston: Houghton, Mifflin and Company. Copyrights 1848, 1876, and 1890. Page 168.

**53.** "I…sat me down…" John Townsend Trowbridge. "The Pewee," lines 53–65. *The Poetical Works of John Townsend Trowbridge.* Boston: Houghton, Mifflin and Company, 1903. Page 14.

**53.** "note with which…" Henry David Thoreau (March 21, 1858).

**53.** "Phe-be…thy call…" Ralph Waldo Emerson. "The Titmouse," lines 94 and 92. *Poems by Ralph Waldo Emerson.* Boston: Houghton, Mifflin and Company, 1904 (first copyright 1867). Page 233.

**53.** "When piped a tiny…" Ralph Waldo Emerson (see above). Lines 26–33. Page 233.

**55.** "There is no…" Ralph Waldo Emerson. Quoted in *The Bird's Calendar* by Howard Elmore Parkhurst. New York: Charles Scribner's Sons, 1894. Page 235.

**56.** "more like a…" Henry David Thoreau (March 5, 1859).

**56.** "no other bird…" John Burroughs. *The Writings of John Burroughs I: Wake Robin.* Boston: Houghton, Mifflin and Company. The Riverside Press, Cambridge. Copyrights 1871, 1876, 1895, 1904, and 1913. Page 213.

**57.** "from a neighboring…" Henry Wadsworth Longfellow. Quoted in *Nestlings of Forest and Marsh* by Irene Grosvenor Wheelock. Chicago: A. C. McClurg and Company, 1902. Page 207.

**57.** "a big noise…" Wells Woodbridge Cooke. "Bird Nomenclature of the Chippewa Indians." Auk, Vol.1, 1884, page 242.

**57.** "You hear…" Henry David Thoreau (February 12, 1854).

**57.** "The Jay he…" Eben Pearson Dorr. Quoted in *Our Friends, the Birds* by Caroline H. Parker. Chicago: A. Flanagan, 1897. Page 27.

**58.** "Besides the ordinary…" Ernest Thompson Seton. *Bird Portraits.* Boston: Ginn and Company, 1901. Page 29.

**58.** "The cawing of…" Bradford Torrey. *Nature's Invitation.* Quoted in *Things Religious and Wild: A Book of Nature Quotations.* Edited by John K. Terres. Fulcrum Publishing, 1991.

**58.** "I heard a great…" Clarence Hawkes. *Tenants of the Trees.* Boston: L. C. Page and Company, 1907. Page 103.

**58.** "The Grackles are…" Clarence Hawkes (see above). Page 102.

**61.** "liquid, bubbling…" Henry David Thoreau (April 22, 1852).

**61.** "The redwing flutes…" Ralph Waldo Emerson. "May-Day." *Poems by Ralph Waldo Emerson.* Boston: Houghton, Mifflin and Company, 1904 (first copyright 1867). Page 163.

**61.** "spent nearly ten…" Louise de Kirline Lawrence. "The Voluble Singer of the Treetops." *Audubon.* May–June 1954.

**62.** "It is the…" William Hamilton Gibson. *Strolls by Starlight and Sunshine.* New York: Harper and Brothers, 1891. Pages 67–68.

**62.** "Do you hear me…" Alice E. Ball. *A Year with the Birds.* New York: Gibbs and Van Vleck, 1916. Page 154.

**62.** "The woods would…" Henry Van Dyke. As quoted in *Reader's Digest,* December 1960, Page 169.

**62.** "It is with birds…" Bradford Torrey. *Birds in the Bush.* Boston: Houghton, Mifflin and Company, 1885. Page 158.

## FLIGHT SONGS AND NIGHT SONGS

**65.** "I hear the…" Henry David Thoreau (June 11, 1851).

**65.** "launches into air…" Henry David Thoreau (May 18, 1860).

**65.** "ecstasy of song…" John Burroughs. *The Writings of John Burroughs I: Wake Robin.* Boston: Houghton, Mifflin and Company. The Riverside Press, Cambridge. Copyrights 1871, 1876, 1895, 1904, and 1913. Page 58.

**66.** "Fair Haven Pond…" Henry David Thoreau (August 5, 1858).

**66.** "Ordinarily, the Meadowlark…" Arthur A. Allen. *Book of Bird Life.* New York: D. Van Nostrand Company, 1930. Page 57.

69. "Once more the..." Benjamin F. Leggett. Quoted in *Our Friends, the Birds* by Caroline H. Parker. Chicago: A. Flanagan, 1897. Page 19.

70. "a grand medley..." Arthur A. Allen. *Book of Bird Life.* New York: D. Van Nostrand Company, 1930. Page 61.

70. "Higher still and..." Percy Bysshe Shelly. "To a Skylark," lines 6–11 (first published in 1820). *The Complete Poetical Works of Percy Bysshe Shelley, Centenary Edition in Four Volumes,* vol. 3. Boston: Houghton, Mifflin and Company, 1892. Page 270.

70. "Hark, hark..." William Shakespeare. Cymbeline, Act II, Scene. iii, line 20 (written circa 1610). Taken from *The Home Book of Quotations: Classical and Modern.* Tenth Edition. Selected and arranged by Burton Stevenson. New York: Dodd, Mead and Company, 1967.

70. "The skylark warbles..." Thomas Gray. "Ode on the Pleasure Arising from Vicissitude," lines 13–16 (written circa 1754). *Thomas Gray and William Collins, Poetical Works.* Edited by Roger Lonsdale. Oxford, London, and New York: Oxford University Press, 1977. Page 59.

70. "The Horned Lark..." Frank Chapman. *Bird Life.* New York: D. Appleton and Company, 1897. Page 160.

72. "his song is..." John Burroughs. *The Writings of John Burroughs I: Wake Robin.* Boston: Houghton, Mifflin and Company. The Riverside Press, Cambridge. Copyrights 1871, 1876, 1895, 1904, and 1913. Page 17.

72. "Nature's minstrel..." Henry David Thoreau (April 25, 1841).

72. "He sits on..." Henry David Thoreau (May 12, 1857).

72. "Upon a pasture..." Edith Thomas. "The Vesper Sparrow." *In Sunshine Land.* Boston: Houghton Mifflin Company, 1894. Page 47.

73. "carols under that..." Walt Whitman. "Out of the Cradle Endlessly Rocking," line 102 (poem first published in 1859). *Leaves of Grass.* Boston: James R. Osgood and Company, 1881. Page 196.

73. "a soft, sweet..." Richard Henry Wilde. "To the Mocking-Bird." *Hesperia: A Poem.* Boston: Ticknor and Fields, 1867. Page 235. Note: "To the Mocking-bird" first printed October 25, 1836 in the *Enquirer* (Richmond, Virginia).

73. "On moonlit nights..." Edward Forbush. *Birds of Massachusetts and other New England States,* vol. 3. Published by the Comonwealth of Massachusetts, 1929. Page 140.

73. "liquid rain..." Anonymous. "To the Catbird." Quoted in *The Bird-Lover's Anthology.* Compiled by Clinton Scollard and Jessie B. Brittenhouse. Boston: Houghton Mifflin Company, 1930. Page 140.

75. "When birds sang..." Henry Wadsworth Longfellow. "Woods in Winter." *The Complete Poetical Works of Henry Wadsworth Longfellow.* Boston: Houghton, Mifflin and Company, 1902. Page 10.

77. "Trills a wild..." Olive Thorne Miller. *With the Birds of Maine.* Boston: Houghton, Mifflin and Company, 1904. Page 86 (Note: this may be a fragment of someone else's poem.)

78. "The low universal..." Henry David Thoreau (June 2, 1853).

81. "The robin is..." Emily Dickinson. "The Robin." *Poems by Emily Dickinson; Second Series.* Edited by Mabel Loomis Todd and T. W. Higginson. Boston: Little, Brown, and Company, 1898 (originally published 1891). Page 117.

81. "The robins sing..." Henry David Thoreau (April 16, 1856).

82. "I hear around..." Henry David Thoreau (June 22, 1852).

84. "Never before had..." Leander Keyser. *In Bird Land.* Chicago: A. C. McClurg and Company, 1897. Page 232.

84. "His voice is..." John Burroughs. *The Writings of John Burroughs I: Wake Robin.* Boston: Houghton, Mifflin and Company. The Riverside Press, Cambridge. Copyrights 1871, 1876, 1895, 1904, and 1913. Page 166.

86. "breaking out as..." Henry David Thoreau (June 11, 1851).

86. "It is an..." Bradford Torrey. *Birds in the Bush.* Boston: Houghton, Mifflin and Company, 1885. Page 43.

86. "There are few..." Reginald Heber Howe. *On the Bird's Highway.* Boston: Sherman, French and Company, 1899. Page 65.

## DAWN CHORUS

89. "In the morning..." Wilson Flagg. *A Year With the Birds; or, The Birds and Seasons of New England.* Boston: Educational Publishing Company, 1881. Page 80.

89. "Early in the..." Wilson Flagg (see above). Page 89.

90. "Nature has so..." Wilson Flagg (see above). Page 47.

91. "The first really..." Henry David Thoreau (July 7, 1852).

93. "The birds sing..." Henry David Thoreau (June 4, 1852).

95. "A thousand birds..." Henry David Thoreau (March 10, 1852).

96. "ambrosial mornings..." Henry David Thoreau (March 10, 1852).

96. "I listen to..." Arthur A. Allen. *Book of Bird Life.* New York: D. Van Nostrand Company, 1930. Page 397.

96. "Think, every morning..." Henry Wadsworth Longfellow. "Tales of a Wayside Inn, The Poet's Tale: Birds of Killingsworth," lines 121–128. *The Complete Poetical Works of Henry Wadsworth Longfellow.* Boston: Houghton, Mifflin and Company, 1902.

## MESSAGES OF THE POETS

99. "A melancholy..." Samuel Taylor Coleridge. "The Nightingale; A Conversational Poem," lines 14–15 (written April 1798). *The Complete Works of Samuel Taylor Coleridge: VII.* New York: Harper and Brothers, 1853. Page 173.

99. "Sparrow singing..." Yosa Buson. *The Essential Haiku: Versions of Basho, Buson, and Issa.* Edited by Robert Hass. Hopewell, New Jersey: The Ecco Press, 1994. Page 87.

99. "As a twig..." James Russel Lowell. "She Came and Went." *The Poetical Works of James Russell Lowell, in Four Volumes: Vol. I.* Boston: Houghton, Mifflin and Company. Copyrights 1848, 1876, and 1890. Page 245.

100. "There is a..." Robert Frost. "The Ovenbird," lines 1–3. *Mountain Interval.* New York: Henry Holt and Company, 1916. Page 35.

100. "deep, secluded..." Walt Whitman. "When Lilacs last in the Dooryard Bloom'd," line 129 (poem first published 1865). *Leaves of Grass.* Boston: James R. Osgood and Company, 1881. Page 255.

100. "deep, solemn..." Emily Tolman. Quoted in *Birds of Song and Story* by Elizabeth and Joseph Grinnell. Chicago: A. W. Mumford, 1901. Page 44.

100. "When God had..." John B. Tabb. "The Bluebird." *Child Verse: Poems Grave and Gay.* Boston: Small, Maynard and Company, 1899. Page 7.

102. "that first note..." John Burroughs. *The Writings of John Burroughs III: Birds and Poets.* Boston: Houghton Mifflin Company. Riverside Press, Cambridge. Copyrights 1877, 1895, and 1904. Page 46.

102. "His soft warble..." Henry David Thoreau (March 2, 1859).

102. "I am excited..." Henry David Thoreau (February 18, 1857).

105. "My bedroom..." Robert Louis Stevenson. Quoted in *With the Birds of Maine* by Olive Thorne Miller. Boston: Houghton Mifflin Company, 1904. Page 251.

105. "What is the..." Henry David Thoreau (February 20, 1857).

106. "The ornithologist..." Joseph Wood Krutch. *The Great Chain of Life*. Boston: Houghton Mifflin Company, 1956. Page 223.

106. "Teach me half..." Percy Bysshe Shelley. "To a Skylark," lines 106–111 (first published in 1820). *The Complete Poetical Works of Percy Bysshe Shelley, Centenary Edition in Four Volumes,* vol. 3. Boston: Houghton, Mifflin and Company, 1892. Page 270.

106. "so of all..." W. Warde Fowler. *Summer Studies of Birds and Books*. London: Macmillan and Company, 1895. Page 124.

106. "Each new year..." Henry David Thoreau (March 10, 1852).

107. "Birdsong brings..." Jelaluddin Rumi (1207–1273). *Birdsong: Fifty-three Short Poems by Rumi*. Translated by Coleman Barks. Athens, Georgia: Maypop, 1993. Page 13.

107. "A light broke..." Lord Byron (George Gordon Byron Baron). *The Prisoner of Chillon*. Geneva: Jullien Freres, Booksellers, 1854 (poem first published in 1816). Page 16.

107. "The little cares..." Elizabeth Barrett Browning. "Out in the Field with God." Quoted in *Bird Day Bulletin*. Department of Game and Fisheries. Birmingham, Alabama: Birmingham Printing Company. March 14, 1930, Page 39.

108. "sing the music..." Kobyashi Issa. *The Essential Haiku: Versions of Basho, Buson, and Issa*. Edited by Robert Hass. Hopewell, New Jersey: The Ecco Press, 1994. Page 221.

108. "Herkneth thise..." Geoffrey Chaucer. "Nun's Priest's Tale," (written circa 1390). *The Canterbury Tales*. From the text of W. W. Skeat. London: Oxford University Press, 1906. Page 258.

108. "For in truth..." Leonardo da Vinci. Source unknown; I found this quote on the internet.

108. "Would not half..." Caroline H. Parker. *Our Friends, the Birds*. Chicago: A. Flanagan, 1897. Page 11.

## SPIRIT OF LISTENING

111. "Lacking the heart-room..." Samuel A. Harper. *Twelve Months with the Birds and Poets*. Chicago: R. F. Seymour. 1917. Page 21.

111. "The music of..." Wilson Flagg. *A Year With the Birds; or, The Birds and Seasons of New England*. Boston: Educational Publishing Company, 1881. Page 8.

111. "And now I..." Arthur A. Allen. *Book of Bird Life*. New York: D. Van Nostrand Company, 1930. Page 397.

112. "What an endless..." William Hamilton Gibson. *Strolls by Starlight and Sunshine*. New York: Harper and Brothers, 1891. Page 64.

112. "Come forth..." William Wordsworth. "The Tables Turned," lines 15–16 (poem written in 1798). *The Complete Poetical Works of William Wordsworth*. Boston: Houghton Mifflin Company, 1904. Page 83.

112. "You hear a..." Bradford Torrey. *Birds in the Bush*. Boston: Houghton, Mifflin and Company, 1885. Page 89.

112. "If I could..." Ralph Waldo Emerson. "My Garden." *Poems by Ralph Waldo Emerson*. Boston: Houghton, Mifflin and Company, 1904 (first copyright 1867). Page 229.

112. "Ornithilogy cannot..." John Burroughs. *The Writings of John Burroughs I: Wake Robin*. Boston: Houghton, Mifflin and Company. The Riverside Press, Cambridge. Copyrights 1871, 1876, 1895, 1904, and 1913. Page 221.

112. "Enough of Science..." William Wordsworth. "The Tables Turned," lines 29–32. (poem written in 1798). *The Complete Poetical Works of William Wordsworth*. Boston and New York: Houghton Mifflin Company. 1904, Page 83.

115. "An incantation..." Henry Van Dyke: "The Maryland Yellowthroat," lines 8–11. *The Builders and other Poems by Henry Van Dyke*. New York: Charles Scribner's Sons, 1897. Page 25.

116. "Of what avail..." Solomon Ibn-Gabirol. Eleventh-century Spanish poet. Quoted in *The Earth Speaks* by Steve Van Matre and Bill Weiler. Warrenville, Illinois: Institute for Earth Education, 1983. Page 131.

116. " 'Tis Eden..." Samuel Harper. *Twelve Months with the Birds and Poets*. Chicago: R. F. Seymour, 1917. Page 20.

116. "Lacking the heart-room..." Samuel Harper (see above). Page 21.

116. "Dear hidden bird..." Christopher Pearse Cranch. "The Song of the Thrush." Quoted in *Our Birds and Their Nestlings* by Margaret Coulson Walker. New York: American Book Company, 1904. Page 148.

117. "Of didst thou..." Ralph Waldo Emerson. "Woodnotes II," lines 249–252. *Poems*. Boston: Phillips, Samson and Company, 1856 (copyright 1846). Page 89.

117. "There is a..." Aldo Leopold. *A Sand County Almanac*. New York: Oxford University Press, 1960 (first copyright 1949). Page 53.

117. "Thrice welcome..." William Wordsworth. "To the Cuckoo," lines 13–16 (poem written in 1804). *The Complete Poetical Works of William Wordsworth*. Boston: Houghton Mifflin Company, 1904. Page 310.

117. "Every bird's voice..." Bradford Torrey. Quoted in *Things Religious and Wild: A Book of Nature Quotations*. Edited by John K. Terres. Fulcrum Publishing, 1991.

119. "songs yet half..." Author unknown. Quoted in *The Wren* by Edward A. Armstrong. London: Collins. 1955. Page 89.

119. "My aviary is..." Clarence Hawkes. *Tenants of the Trees*. Boston: L. C. Page and Company, 1907. Page 2.

120. "How watchful..." Henry David Thoreau (October 26, 1853).

133. "Bury me where..." Alexander Wilson. Quoted in *The American Treasury: 1455–1955*. Edited by Clifton Fadiman. New York: Harper and Brothers, Publishers, 1955. Quote dated August 23, 1813.

*Yellow Warbler*

# Sources: Scientific References

The references listed below are modern scientific books on bird song and communication. For a list of scientific journal articles that the author consulted in writing this book, visit the author's Web site at *www.naturesound.com* and follow the link to the *Music of the Birds* Web page.

Armstrong, E. A. *A Study of Bird Song.* New York: Dover, 1963. An early classic book on bird song.

Catchpole, C. K, and P. J. B. Slater. *Bird Song: Biological Themes and Variations.* Cambridge, England: Cambridge University Press, 1995. Highly recommended: a recent summary of scientific knowledge.

Hartshorne, C. *Born to Sing.* Bloomington: Indiana University Press, 1973. Written by a philospher turned ornithologist; birds of the world are ranked according to their singing abilities.

Jellis, R. *Bird Sounds and Their Meaning.* London: British Broadcasting Corporation, 1977. An excellent introduction to bird sound, written primarily for the layperson.

Kroodsma, D. E., and E. H. Miller, editors. *Acoustic Communication in Birds.* 2 volumes. New York: Academic Press, 1982. An authoritative collection of nineteen chapters written by prominent ornithologists.

————, editors. *Ecology and Evolution of Acoustic Communication in Birds.* Ithaca, New York: Cornell University Press, 1996. An excellent collection of twenty-six chapters surveying modern research.

Morton, E. S., and J. Page. *Animal Talk.* New York: Random House, 1992. Co-written by an ornithologist and science writer; introduces new ideas about the evolution of animal communication.

Smith, W. J. *The Behavior of Communicating: An Ethological Approach.* Cambridge: Harvard University Press, 1977. A fine introduction to animal communication in general.

Thorpe, W. H. *Bird Song.* Cambridge, England: Cambridge University Press, 1961. An early scientific review of research on bird song.

*Bury me where the birds*
*will sing over my grave*
—ALEXANDER WILSON

*Eastern Towhee*

# Index to Species

*Accepted common names are listed alphabetically, with page number references*

*Rose-breasted Grosbeak*

## LIMITED EDITION PRINTS

Selected images from this book are available as signed and numbered limited edition *Giclée* art prints. For more information, visit the author's Web site at *www.naturesound.com,* or write NatureSound Studio, P.O. Box 84, Ithaca, New York 14851-0084.

## SONGBIRD PORTRAITS CD

A special audio compact disc is available featuring songbird solos and choruses recorded in full stereo without narration—a full hour of pure listening pleasure. Many of our most talented native songsters are included. For more information, visit the author's Web site at *www.naturesound.com,* write NatureSound Studio at P.O. Box 84, Ithaca, New York 14851-0084, or phone your order using your credit card: 1-800-225-3362.